T0191173

Does the Jewish Bible Point to Jesus? Here is a book that takes you through some key Jewish Bible texts and offers what many may find a surprising conclusion. Written in a clear style, this book will reveal the clues God has left in His Word for what He is doing in the midst of our needy world.
DARRELL L. BOCK, Executive Director for Cultural Engagement Hendricks Center, Senior Research Professor of New Testament Studies

If you love the Jewish people and God's plan for them, as well as His plan for all people, then you will be thrilled to read this marvelous book by David Brickner. He does a brilliant job of taking twelve key prophecies in Hebrew Scripture (the Old Testament) and demonstrating how they have been fulfilled in the life of Yeshua. Though these twelve prophecies might be considered by some people to be complex or complicated, David Brickner does a superb job of explaining them with easy-to-understand clarity. I can't say enough about the value of this work. It is a treasure to read and a treasure to be shared!
BRYAN HUGHES, Senior Pastor of Grace Bible Church in Bozeman, MT, and author of *Romans 8:28 and Jesus's Teaching on the Last Days*

"Does the Jewish Bible point to Jesus?" This question is one that is repeatedly asked among our people, especially in times when anti-Semitism raises its ugly head. Yet, during such challenges, our people often discover that the best friends our people can count on are those who believe in the Scriptures and who find therein the foundation of their faith thanks to Messiah. Nowadays we more clearly observe that love for Israel among Christians is a gift bestowed supernaturally from God for those who cherish the Word of God and who understand the place of Israel in God's plan of salvation. Therefore, it is especially important for those who really love the Jewish people to know how they should present the love of God that is found in Messiah-Yeshua in a way that is accessible, and not in a manner foreign to our people. David did a wonderful job in answering the question of the title of his book, both to Jewish and Gentile audiences alike.
SAMUEL SMADJA, Owner & President, Sar-El Group

David Brickner has written such an engaging book! It's like walking through space and time, encountering Moses and the prophets of old as they charted the path of the coming Messiah long before his appearance. Into his study of the Tanakh, Brickner artfully weaves the stories of many contemporary Jews who encountered a living hope in its pages: the hope of Israel.
FLORENT VARAK, Chairman of the European Board of Jews for Jesus and senior director at Encompass World Partners

I am thrilled to recommend David Brickner's newest title, *Does the Jewish Bible Point to Jesus?* For anyone serious about reaching Jewish people with the message of Messiah, and for anyone seeking the truth of God's promised Deliverer, Yeshua, this book is a must-read.
MARK M. YARBROUGH, President and Professor of Bible Exposition, Dallas Theological Seminary; author of *How to Read the Bible Like a Seminary Professor*

From the Law of Moses to the Prophets, and the Psalms, Jesus is there. David brilliantly takes twelve prophecies from these three groupings of Scripture to illustrate how the Old Testament cannot be "disconnected" from the New Testament. This book will remind you that Jesus came and is coming again, so "that the Scripture might be fulfilled." May your heart be filled with encouragement and joyous anticipation as you discover how the Bible points to Jesus, right from the start.
JANET PARSHALL, nationally syndicated talk show host

This book offers an easy-to-read discussion about the Messiah in the Hebrew Bible from a Jewish man who has spent decades thinking about this topic. This book is a great read for a reader who is considering the topic of the Messiah in the Hebrew Bible for the first time, as well as the reader who has been thinking about this for years.
SETH POSTELL, Lecturer in Biblical Studies at Israel College of the Bible in Netanya, Israel

In *Does the Jewish Bible Point to Jesus?*, David Brickner opens his Jewish Bible to help us all see Jesus of Nazareth there—in the Law, the Prophets, and the Writings. If you doubt that the Hebrew Scriptures, taken on their own terms, really point to Jesus, this book can satisfy your reservations.
RAY ORTLUND, Renewal Ministries, Nashville, TN

At last! David Brickner, the long-time leader of Jews for Jesus, lays out the Messianic claims of Jesus (Yeshua), based on Old Testament prophecy in a way that every reader can grasp. This helpful book is as edifying as it is practical. Read if you love the Jewish Messiah and the Jewish people.
MICHAEL L. BROWN, host of the *Line of Fire* radio broadcast; author of the five-volume series *Answering Jewish Objections to Jesus*; and the Director of Spiritual Renewal and Apologetics at the Jerusalem Bible Institute

David Brickner's *Does the Jewish Bible Point to Jesus?* presents a thought-provoking examination of key prophetic passages and offers consequential insights for all readers. Written in a relatable and contextualized manner, Brickner challenges readers to engage deeply with the prophetic texts for themselves. For anyone seeking clarity on this issue, Brickner's voice emerges as compelling, timely, and indispensable. *Does the Jewish Bible Point to Jesus?* represents Brickner's lifelong commitment to studying these texts, resulting in an essential resource for today's seekers and believers alike.
DOMINICK S. HERNANDEZ, associate professor of Old Testament and Semitics at Talbot School of Theology, Biola University

The Messiahship of Yeshua is a topic of much misunderstanding in the Jewish (and non-Jewish) world. Through an authentic Jewish conversation, David Brickner explains in an engaging and personal way to both Jewish and Gentile readers how Yeshua fits the criteria of the promised Messiah, while making the good news very clear along the journey. The book starts with a vivid description of the resurrection of the Messiah, and then weaves through the Tenach, the Hebrew Scriptures, unpacking the passages that speak of who this Messiah would be and what he would do. This book has been an exciting read and I believe it will have a great impact on whoever reads it, whether they believe in Yeshua or not.
EREZ SOREF, President of ONE FOR ISRAEL; author of articles and books, including *Reading Moses, Seeing Jesus: How the Torah Fulfills Its Goal in Yeshua*

DOES THE JEWISH BIBLE POINT TO JESUS?

12 Key Prophecies That Unfold God's Plan

David Brickner

MOODY PUBLISHERS

CHICAGO

© 2024 by
DAVID BRICKNER

All rights reserved. No part of this book may be reproduced in any form without permission in writing from the publisher, except in the case of brief quotations embodied in critical articles or reviews.

All Scripture quotations, unless otherwise indicated, are taken from the New King James Version. Copyright © 1982, 1992 by Thomas Nelson, Inc. Used by permission. All rights reserved.

Scripture quotations marked (NIV) are taken from the Holy Bible, New International Version®, NIV®. Copyright © 1973, 1978, 1984, 2011 by Biblica, Inc.™ Used by permission of Zondervan. All rights reserved worldwide. www.zondervan.com The "NIV" and "New International Version" are trademarks registered in the United States Patent and Trademark Office by Biblica, Inc.™

Scripture quotations marked NASB are taken from the (NASB®) New American Standard Bible®, Copyright © 1960, 1971, 1977, 1995, 2020 by The Lockman Foundation. Used by permission. All rights reserved. lockman.org

Scripture quotations marked (ESV) are from the ESV® Bible (The Holy Bible, English Standard Version®), © 2001 by Crossway, a publishing ministry of Good News Publishers. Used by permission. All rights reserved. The ESV text may not be quoted in any publication made available to the public by a Creative Commons license. The ESV may not be translated in whole or in part into any other language.

Scripture quotations marked (NLT) are taken from the Holy Bible, New Living Translation, copyright ©1996, 2004, 2015 by Tyndale House Foundation. Used by permission of Tyndale House Publishers, Carol Stream, Illinois 60188. All rights reserved.

Some names and story details changed to protect the privacy of individuals.

Edited by Cheryl Molin
Interior design: Ragont Design
Cover design: Thinkpen Design
Cover graphic of arrow copyright © 2024 by Receh Lancar Jaya/Shutterstock (1673804221). All rights reserved.

Library of Congress Cataloging-in-Publication Data

Names: Brickner, David N., author.
Title: Does the Jewish Bible point to Jesus? : 12 key prophecies that
   unfold God's plan / by David N. Brickner.
Description: Chicago, IL : Moody Publishers, 2024. | Includes
   bibliographical references. | Summary: "Messianic Jewish author David
   Brickner guides us through twelve prophecies from the Old Testament.
   Whether you're curious, skeptical, or a committed believer, this book is
   for you. Come and see how God's timeless plan to redeem and renew the
   world still shines as a beacon of hope today"-- Provided by publisher.
Identifiers: LCCN 2024012716 (print) | LCCN 2024012717 (ebook) | ISBN
   9780802434166 (paperback) | ISBN 9780802470904 (ebook)
Subjects: LCSH: Bible. Old Testament--Prophecies. | Jesus Christ--Jewish
   interpretations. | Messiah. | Bible. New Testament--Relation to the Old
   Testament. | BISAC: RELIGION / Judaism / General | RELIGION / Biblical
   Studies / Old Testament / General
Classification: LCC BS1198 .B63166 2024 (print) | LCC BS1198 (ebook) |
   DDC 232/.12--dc23/eng/20240512
LC record available at https://lccn.loc.gov/2024012716
LC ebook record available at https://lccn.loc.gov/2024012717

Originally delivered by fleets of horse-drawn wagons, the affordable paperbacks from D. L. Moody's publishing house resourced the church and served everyday people. Now, after more than 125 years of publishing and ministry, Moody Publishers' mission remains the same—even if our delivery systems have changed a bit. For more information on other books (and resources) created from a biblical perspective, go to www.moodypublishers.com or write to:

Moody Publishers
820 N. LaSalle Boulevard
Chicago, IL 60610

1 3 5 7 9 10 8 6 4 2

Printed in the United States of America

This book is dedicated to my parents, Avi and Leah Brickner, whose love for God and His Word has provided the foundation and inspiration for my own spiritual trajectory.

Contents

Foreword

Paul, one of the first-century Jews for Jesus, used to visit synagogues on the Sabbath and reason with people from the Scriptures, that "this Jesus whom I preach to you is the [Messiah]" (Acts 17:1–3). What Scriptures did Paul use to make his case for Jesus? The same Scriptures that Jesus himself used: the Jewish Bible, also known as the Old Testament.

Examining the Jewish Scriptures was and still is a powerful way for Jews and Gentiles to understand who Jesus is and what he can mean to them personally. Without the Jewish Scriptures, we have no basis for understanding why God promised a Messiah, let alone what the Messiah was to accomplish. Nor would we know the many details by which the Jewish people (or anyone else) could recognize the Messiah. In other words, the Jewish Bible is the God-given context of the messianic hope, and it provides the necessary criteria for evaluating anyone who claims (as Jesus did) to fulfill that hope.

Context is crucial to any serious consideration of Jesus, and that is exactly what this book provides. Whether you are trying to decide what to believe about Jesus, or whether you hope to deepen and share the faith you already have in him, take this opportunity to explore his life, death, and resurrection from the most compelling context: prophecies that were written hundreds of years before he walked the earth.

In *Does the Jewish Bible Point to Jesus?*, David traces the messianic hope through every section of the Old Testament. He not only unpacks the Scriptures, but he also gives historical context, biblical nuances, illustrations, and personal glimpses into how others have responded to these prophecies. He neither assumes that his readers share his beliefs, nor presses them to do so. Rather, he encourages them to ponder what the Scriptures might be saying to them.

Admittedly, my praise for this book has a personal component. Like David, I am a Jewish believer in Jesus, committed to helping my people consider Jesus from a biblical perspective. That commitment drew me, as it also drew David, to Jews for Jesus. As a member of their board of directors for years, I came to know David well, particular during his tenure as Jews for Jesus Executive Director from September 1996–June 2024. We continue to work together as he now serves as the Executive Chairman of the board.

David and I have both been privileged to share with many thousands of people what the Bible has to say about God's plan to heal this broken world. David has done this through the auspices of Jews for Jesus, whereas I've spent more than fifty years as lead pastor of McLean Bible Church. I've invited David to speak at McLean many times. I could always count on him to share biblical insights—life-changing insights—in an engaging and dynamic way while staying faithful and true to the text. You can count on him to do the same in this book. May God bless you as you read it.

Lon Solomon
Senior Pastor Emeritus, McLean Bible Church, McLean, VA
President and Founder, Lon Solomon Ministries

Opened Minds Open Up Possibilities

When Ellen, a Jewish musician, attended a concert of Handel's *Messiah*, she found herself surprisingly moved. She was eager to discuss her experience with Laura Barron, a Jewish believer in Jesus.

"You should go hear Handel's *Messiah*," Ellen told Laura. "I think you'd like it because it's all about Jesus, based on the New Testament."

Laura smiled. "What if I told you that more than half the lyrics to that piece are from the Jewish Bible (also known as the Hebrew Scriptures or Old Testament)?"

"But they must be from the New Testament! I know the piece is about Jesus; it was so specific and detailed."

"You're right," Laura agreed, "it *is* about Jesus, and some of the words *are* from the New Testament. But Handel's *Messiah* includes even more passages from the Jewish Bible—from Isaiah 7, Isaiah 53, Psalm 2, and Psalm 22—just to name a few!"

As Laura went through several of the passages with her, Ellen was astounded. Not only had it never occurred to her that the Jewish Bible would be pointing to Yeshua (Jesus), but its predictions about who the Messiah would be and what he would do were positively mind-boggling. Ellen's response was understandable . . . and not at all uncommon.[1]

Even Jesus' first disciples, the ones who traveled with him for three years, found it difficult to wrap their minds around his identity and his mission. Imagine how you would feel if you had been his student and his friend. You've heard his teachings, seen his miracles, and now you can't wait to watch him defeat the Romans and set up his kingdom. Instead, you watch him die, executed by the very soldiers you expected him to conquer. Why in the world would you spend the rest of your life telling people to believe in him? You wouldn't, and neither would those disciples . . . if this hadn't happened:

A Defining Moment for Jesus' First Disciples

The dark, narrow room wasn't meant for so many people, yet the air was not oppressive but electric with a mix of fear and wonder. Dim light revealed a gathering of mostly men, bearded and robed. No one knew quite what to make of the news from the people who had claimed to see Jesus three days after he'd been crucified. But something was about to happen; they could feel it. And suddenly the moment of silent anticipation was broken by startled gasps.

He had appeared out of nowhere. The group pressed in closer to him, amazed as he showed them his nail-scarred hands and feet—yet terrified. Was he a ghost? But when he asked, "Is there something to eat?" they gave him a piece of broiled fish and he ate it right in front of them. A ghost doesn't do that. Maybe there were even a few bones left on the plate, but the evidence was incontrovertible. Yeshua (Jesus) was alive and real and standing in their midst!

They had watched him die on a Roman cross just a few days earlier. They knew where he had been buried—in the tomb of a rich man named Joseph. They'd heard the tomb was empty . . . some had gone to see for themselves. And now Jesus stood before them alive and in person, and the world would never be the same. How had this happened and what did it all mean? They were about to find out.

"Then he [Yeshua] said to them, 'These are my words that I spoke to you while I was still with you, that everything written about me in the Law of Moses and the Prophets and the Psalms must be fulfilled.'[2] Then he opened their minds to understand the Scriptures" (Luke 24:44–45 ESV).

I would love to have been a fly on the wall when Yeshua appeared. I wish I could have heard how he opened their minds to understand what had been written of him in the Law, the Prophets, and the Psalms. One thing is certain. That first group of Jewish believers in Jesus experienced something powerful *after his crucifixion*—something so convincing that it shaped the rest of their lives and changed the course of history. Whatever doubts they may have had were thoroughly overcome by their certainty that he was alive again[3]—and they were willing to die rather than keep quiet about it.

Experiences Fade but God's Word Doesn't

Yeshua knew that it was hugely important for his disciples to see with their own eyes that he had come back from the grave. But he also knew that their own experience would not be enough for the long road that lay ahead. In years to come, difficult circumstances might darken the distant memory of his physical presence, but his teachings from the Jewish Bible would remain bright and clear.

The wonderful thing about God is that, time and time again, he speaks a word of hope in the darkest of times. The Scriptures give evidence of that. That's why Yeshua did not merely pop in for a little *nosh* (bite to eat)—though I can tell you from experience that food is an important part of most Jewish events. He opened their minds to the solid, unchanging, hope-giving words of the Hebrew Scriptures, not just for their own understanding, but to share with others. Those words would shine as a bright light no matter how dark the circumstances might become. What's more, the disciples would be inspired to write the New Testament, passing on that light for generations of future followers who would not have experienced Yeshua's physical presence.

Messiah in the *Tanakh*

We don't know which passages Jesus talked about as he opened their minds to the realities of his life and mission. But we do know that he was speaking from the *Tanakh*. Tanakh is an acrostic for the three portions of the Hebrew Scriptures: the *Torah* (Law of Moses), *Nevi'im* (the Prophets), and the *Ketuvim* (the Writings, which includes books such as the Psalms).

This book will walk you through a sampling of twelve prophecies from those three groupings of Scripture. I hope they will increase your appetite for more.

As you work your way through these prophecies, may God use them to open your mind to the plans he laid long before Jesus walked the earth. May you find that Yeshua's fulfillment of these prophecies points to a love so astonishing and powerful that it can open not only your mind, but your heart as well.

If you are already a believer, I pray that these mind-opening Scriptures will fill you with a fresh sense of the supernatural nature of God's Word and renew your hope and your confidence to share your faith with those you care about. Just as Jesus equipped his first disciples to go and tell others, so he wants to equip those of us who are his disciples today.

Wherever you may be on your faith journey, may your mind be opened to the life-changing, hope-giving power offered through the Messiah, and all he did in order "that the Scriptures might be fulfilled."

Clues About Messiah in the Torah

The Torah—the five books of Moses—is the foundational document of the Jewish people. Judaism looks to the Torah for its laws and commandments. Yet within the Torah Jews and Christians alike find the story of humanity's origins, the entrance of sin and evil into the universe, and most importantly, God's promises to redeem our broken world.

In this section we look at key passages from Genesis 3, Genesis 12, Genesis 49, and Deuteronomy 18. As we explore these passages, the promise of redemption—initially enigmatic—begins to take clearer shape. For the story of redemption is bound up with the descendants of Abraham, Isaac, and Jacob, from the tribe of Judah in particular, and with a "prophet like Moses" who was yet to come at the time the Torah was given. Thus the Jewish people end up "front and center" in God's plan to redeem the world.

*"And I will put enmity
Between you and the woman,
And between your seed and her Seed;
He shall bruise your head,
And you shall bruise His heel."*

Genesis 3:15

Messiah will come from the seed of the woman.

CHAPTER 1

Why a Messiah?

My wife and I frequently have houseguests, and on one occasion we hosted a family that included an adorable three-year-old named Levi. He was curious about everything he saw—everything in our home was new and thought-provoking to him. And he kept asking me, "Why? Why? Why?" I found myself explaining why our dog Nola barked, why my hot tub water was hot, why the toast popped up out of my toaster, etc. I appreciated Levi's questions and his hunger for understanding.

Sadly, as we grow older and busier, it's easy to become less reflective about life. Our desire to understand life's "whys" can be dampened by disappointment and disillusionment.

Don't Stop Asking

When was the last time you seriously wondered, "What is wrong with the world? Why all the pain and suffering?" and then actually tried to discover the answer? It only takes a glance at the daily news to provoke that question, but many have either stopped asking or have accepted prepackaged explanations. Politicians are especially good at blaming the opposition for all our problems, yet no matter who is in power, they are unable to prevent the pain and loss we all face at some point. Maybe it's a shattered relationship, the death of a loved one, a debilitating accident or illness, a broken heart for those suffering from war and poverty, or even an inexplicable sense of emptiness.

If we resign ourselves to the idea that "this is just the way things are," we miss out on what could be. If we will open our minds to discovering the genesis of what has gone wrong in our world, God will show us his plan to make it right.

Whatever is wrong with the world, it is certainly not a new phenomenon. Jesus' early followers might well have wondered what went wrong after their hopes had been dashed as they watched him die on that Roman cross. But his astonishing return to life revealed that what had seemed like the ultimate defeat was the ultimate victory—a fulfillment of God's plan to fix what is wrong with the world.

The Problem and the Promise

The promise of a Messiah is inseparably intertwined with the root of all our problems—and so the problem and the promise both began to unfold at the very dawn of human history.

We see the first prophetic prediction of Messiah in the beginning chapters of the Torah, in Genesis 3:15.

> "And I will put enmity
> Between you and the woman,
> And between your seed and her Seed;

He shall bruise your head,
And you shall bruise His heel."

The context of this prophecy is the very first Bible narrative about human life, known as the story of the Garden of Eden. Most have heard this story. The first man and woman, Adam and Eve, were living in an exquisite garden that offered everything they needed to thrive, prepared for them by God himself. They were free to enjoy this garden paradise with one small provision: the fruit of one tree, the tree of the knowledge of good and evil, was off-limits to them. God warned that the penalty for eating the fruit would be death.

Did the Punishment Fit the Crime?

Some may shrug or shake their heads at this, thinking the punishment far outweighed what might not seem like much of a crime. But it makes perfect sense if we see that the issue was not stealing a piece of fruit but rejecting God's authority. Eating the fruit would essentially be telling God, "We don't really believe you are the all-knowing, all-powerful, and loving God who has every right to set boundaries—and who does so for our good."

If Adam and Eve were unwilling to trust and obey the Giver of Life who knew exactly what they needed to thrive, how could their lives be sustainable? Death would be inevitable. The crime and the punishment were actually two sides of the same coin—rejection of God.

Sadly, Eve did not resist the temptation to taste the forbidden fruit. She believed the devil, who appeared to her in the form of a serpent. He did not merely offer her the fruit, but told her that God's warning was untrue, and insinuated that it was intended to hold her back from the life she deserved. She gave in to distrust, and disobedience quickly followed. Adam did not refuse when she offered the fruit to him, and together they violated the only stipulation God had given them.

This event, often referred to as "the fall," is the context for the Genesis 3:15 prophecy. God was addressing the serpent immediately after Adam and Eve had fallen to his temptation—and they overheard it all.

Hope Shines in the Dark

God was speaking into the darkest hour of their experience. All the innocence and all the goodness that God had given Adam and Eve and, by extension, the human race, seemed lost forever.

God was about to banish the couple from the Garden of Eden. He was about to tell them how their choice had spoiled much more than the intimacy they'd shared with him. Their lack of trust in God would infect their relationship with each other. They would face insecurity and oppression as husband and wife. Their rejection of God's authority would affect their work, their living conditions—and pretty much all of nature. How could it not? Our experience of paradise comes apart at the seams when we pull away from the God who created it.

But before God pronounces these dark consequences to Adam and Eve, he speaks to the serpent, the one who had deceived them. And as he does, he gives this prophecy as a ray of hope to humanity.

Once again, God says,

"I will put enmity between you [the serpent] and the woman [Eve], and between your offspring and her offspring; he shall bruise your head, and you shall bruise his heel" (Genesis 3:15 ESV).

How is this a ray of hope? How does it predict the solution to what is wrong with the world? It's all about the offspring.

The Mysterious Seed

The word "offspring" in the Hebrew is *zera*, or seed. In other passages, the word *zera* is used to describe the essential male contribution to conceiving life. But in this promise, God specifically describes this future offspring as the seed of the woman! (For more on the meaning of this surprising turn of phrase see chapter 5.)

Somehow *her* offspring is going to be connected uniquely to the birth of someone who will bruise or crush the serpent's head. Several (though not all) English translations say "bruise," but in the Septuagint, the ancient Greek translation of the Hebrew Bible, the passage reads, "He shall crush your head."[1]

How do you kill a snake? You crush its head. Normally you would pick up a weapon to do this; it's too risky to try to kill a serpent by stepping on its head. If you try to step on a poisonous snake, you most likely will be bitten.

Yet it seems that is exactly what the seed of the woman will do: crush the head of the serpent underfoot. And in the process of this crushing, his heel is going to be bruised or crushed as well. I take that to mean he will be bitten by the snake, a mortal wound.

We see in this promise that someone is going to come and put an end to the serpent, defeating the one who introduced the enmity that caused the fall and led to all the brokenness that resulted. The conquering hero would be the seed or offspring of a woman. Yet in the process of defeating Satan, the offspring would himself suffer a mortal wound.[2]

The word "Messiah" is not mentioned in Genesis 3:15; however, his coming is the piece that is needed to make sense of the story. That is why from early times, Jewish literature interpreted this passage as a promise of the Messiah. One of the Targums (ancient paraphrases of the Scriptures in Aramaic) relates this verse to the Messiah.[3]

It makes sense that some Jewish traditions identified the offspring of the woman as none other than the promised Messiah, the one in whom all our best hopes for the future rest. And it is likely that Yeshua's early followers had heard and read that the promised Messiah was the one who would crush the head of their satanic adversary, but they hadn't yet understood how it was to occur.

Jesus opened their minds to see how he fulfilled this ancient promise. His death took on a new meaning as the seed of the woman who would bruise or crush the serpent's head . . . and so he began to reverse the curse from the Garden of Eden at the cost of his life.

In fact, Jesus' death was part of the very proof they needed to see that he was exactly who he claimed to be. His death crushed the plans of the adversary in a way that he never could have had he simply fulfilled his disciples' hopes and expectations. Jesus was able to restore the most precious thing that had been broken: the hope of a relationship between God and humanity.

Jesus would continue to share much more to open his disciples' minds, such as how and why Messiah's death had the power to redeem his people. We will continue to explore passages from the Jewish Scriptures, looking at passages I believe Jesus shared with his followers to help them put it all together. And as they put together the true meaning and scope of what Jesus had done, they were so filled with joy over the good news that they began to proclaim it in Israel and around the world.

Echoes of Genesis 3:15

At key points in the New Testament, we find allusions to Genesis 3:15. For example,

But when the fullness of time had come, God sent forth his Son, born of woman. (Gal. 4:4 ESV)

The God of peace will soon crush Satan under your feet. The grace of our Lord Jesus Christ be with you. (Rom. 16:20 ESV)

An early letter to Jewish followers of Jesus talks about him coming in the flesh so that through his own death, he could destroy Satan: "Since therefore the children share in flesh and blood, he himself likewise partook of the same things, that through death he might destroy the one who has the power of death, that is, the devil" (Heb. 2:14 ESV).

In Revelation, the very last book of the Bible, there is an allusion to a future and final war against "the offspring of the woman," which will finish the crushing of Satan for good.

And the great dragon was thrown down, that ancient serpent, who is called the devil and Satan, the deceiver of the whole world—he was thrown down to the earth, and his angels were thrown down with him. (Rev. 12:9 ESV)

Then the dragon became furious with the woman and went off to make war on the rest of her offspring, on those who keep the commandments of God and hold to the testimony of Jesus. (Rev. 12:17 ESV)

Hope springs forth as a desperately needed light in the darkest of hours, and that's exactly what Genesis 3:15 does. This prophecy provides the first of many strokes that, together, present a wonderful portrait of the one who was promised from the very beginning—the seed of the woman, the Messiah.

Hope for Today

And today? The brokenness introduced by Satan's deception continues. People still believe lies about what God is like and reject his wise boundaries. As a result, we are all busy being deceived, deceiving ourselves and others, and covering up who we really are. But it doesn't have to be that way.

What is your hope in the darkness? The announcement of good news that came at the dawn of human history can still cut through the darkness we experience today. But it requires us to reject the deception, not only about God, but about ourselves.

I've heard it said that a newspaper article once invited readers to write an answer to the question "What is wrong with the world?" G. K. Chesterton purportedly wrote in reply:

"Dear Sir: Regarding your article 'What is Wrong with the World?' I am. Yours truly."

AND YOU?

I have come to the same realization as Chesterton. Have you? If you haven't, would you be willing to consider that we all reject God in one way or another, and have suffered the dehumanizing effects of doing so? It's liberating to be able to see and admit it. Because once we open our minds to our own part in what is wrong with the world, we can open our minds to the solution.

Now the LORD had said to Abram:
"Get out of your country,
From your family
And from your father's house,
To a land that I will show you.
I will make you a great nation;
I will bless you
And make your name great;
And you shall be a blessing.
I will bless those who bless you,
And I will curse him who curses you;
And in you all the families of the earth shall be blessed."

Genesis 12:1–3

Messiah would be a descendant of Abraham.

CHAPTER 2

Get Out . . . and Be Blessed!

Everyone has a story, but sometimes we need a little help to uncover it. Genetic testing through Ancestry.com or 23andMe makes it easy to discover more about our past, and particularly our family heritage. But DNA is only part of the story. A trustworthy record of events can shed light, not only on our own story, but on the stories of those whose footsteps we may choose to follow.

The desire to know where we come from seems to be a holy impulse, and the Bible is full of genealogies that punctuate that desire with a divine exclamation point. The Bible's lists of "begets" emphasize God's strategic plan to place people in families—families that connect us to the past and link us to the future.

God promised a Messiah who would come to redeem and renew the whole world from the brokenness described in Genesis 3. His plan to heal the world was not revealed all at once, but through a series of promises and predictions. Separately these are random clues, but they fit together to paint a picture of the messianic hope. And several of the clues focus on giving birth.

Genesis 3:15 gave us the first clue about the Messiah's identity as the seed of the woman, and it hints at his mission to overcome the one who introduced evil into the world. God makes it clear that he is not going to throw down a lightning bolt from heaven to rescue humanity. He is going to use flesh and blood.

Messiah's Mishpochah

The second major clue about the Messiah's identity reveals that he would come from a branch of Abraham's descendants: the Jewish people. If you are Jewish, you are connected, through your *mishpochah* (Hebrew word for family), to God's ancient promises of a Messiah.

A Pattern of Light in the Darkness

The promise of the messianic blessing in Genesis 12:3, like the promise in Genesis 3:15, comes as a ray of hope in a dark hour. To set the scene, let me recap.

As the book of Genesis opens, God is introduced, and the story of human origins unfolds. God creates man and woman in his image—he made us to be like him. The serpent's great deception is to twist that truth and persuade Eve and Adam that the best way to be like God is to make a grab for self-sufficiency through an act of disobedience. They fall for the lie and end up getting exactly the opposite of what the serpent promised. They become disconnected from God, and in many ways disconnected from each other, and even from their own humanity.

As the book of Genesis continues, we see how the dignity and nobility that God ingrained in men and women is compromised and often obscured by selfish instincts. People are prone to shame, blame, jealousy, distrust, and violence. Death by fratricide results as Cain kills his brother Abel in Genesis 4. By chapter 6, the shadow of the serpent's deception seems to have covered the earth. The evil is so full-blown and the "fruit" of rebelling against God is so toxic that God decides to wash away the entire mess with a massive flood. He spares one faithful man, Noah, and his family to make a fresh start and repopulate the world. Following the flood, God puts a special blessing on one of Noah's sons, Shem.

Humanity Divided in a Grab for Power

By chapter 11, it is clear that the fresh start has gone south. The new population is still afflicted by the old disorder—trying to be like God in all the wrong ways. This reality is dramatically illustrated in the dark story of the Tower of Babel.

As the story unfolds, people are united in a scheme to build a tower "whose top is in the heavens" to "make a name" for themselves and avoid being "scattered abroad" (Gen. 11:4). As with the forbidden fruit, on the surface it may seem like a harmless endeavor. Yet both Jewish and Christian interpretations recognize this effort as a power play.[1] The people were aiming to ensure their own reputation and sovereignty, on par with—and in some rabbinic interpretations, in opposition to—God.

In response, God confuses their language, the people scatter, and before long, nations are against nations. The Tower of Babel amplifies the backstory of brokenness in a world where turning against God causes people to turn against one another.

The post-flood society has shown that a "do-over" will not fix humanity's problem, and now God begins to reveal a bit more of his plan. He's going to use one of Shem's descendants to raise up a family to help fulfill his promise in Genesis 3:15. Through this family, God will ultimately fulfill his promise to bring *tikkun olam* (Hebrew for "repairing the world") to redeem and restore all that is broken. And that family of "Shemites" (from which we get the word "Semite") begins with Abram (later renamed Abraham).

What do we know about Abram? Apparently, he came from a family of idol worshipers. According to *Genesis Rabbah* 38, a *midrash* (compilation of Torah expositions that includes many stories), Abram's father made and sold idols for a living. It's not as though the family had any special claim on God's favor. Still, God speaks to Abram, and once again, his speech is a ray of hope. It pierces the darkness of humanity's alienation from God.

The Big Blessing

God's speech begins with a command to get out and get away from all that is familiar: Abram is to leave his home and his father. God does not give him any destination other than "the land that I will show you." And then God makes a three-part promise to Abram in what is known as the Abrahamic Covenant.

First: "I will make you a great nation" (Gen. 12:2).

Second: "I will bless you and make your name great" (also Gen. 12:2).

Third: "In you all the families of the earth shall be blessed" (Gen. 12:3).

Ironically, God promises to do for Abraham what the ill-fated tower builders had attempted to do for themselves. This was not only ironic but appeared literally inconceivable—Abraham was in his seventies, and his wife, Sarah, was in her sixties and had been proven barren. And, as though to make certain everyone would know this birth was a miracle, the baby was not conceived for another twenty years.

God saves the climax of the promise for last: "In you all the families of the earth shall be blessed" (Gen. 12:3).

God reaffirms this promise in Genesis 18, saying, "Shall I hide from Abraham what I am about to do, seeing that Abraham shall surely become a great and mighty nation, and all the nations of the earth shall be blessed in him?" (vv. 17–18 ESV).

Faith Leads to Obedience

And how does Abraham respond? He believes God. And because he believes, he obeys. He and his wife and nephew and their entourage pack up and head out to who knows where—and Abraham and Sarah end up becoming the patriarch and matriarch of the Jewish people . . . from whom the Jewish Messiah would one day come.

Abraham and Sarah's story is remarkable, not so much because of who they are at the start, but because of who God was, is, and always will be.

If you follow the life of Abraham through the Bible, you see some less-than-great moments. When he gets scared, he hides his true relationship with his wife and turns her over to Pharaoh. And it's not a one-off moment of weakness because he does the same thing later in his life. When God says, "I will make your name great," it's not because Abraham was the greatest guy in the world; it's because in a world of people who all mess up in one way or another, God is great enough to confer greatness on whomever he chooses. The wonderful thing is that even with all his flaws, Abraham was known as God's friend (2 Chron. 20:7; Isa. 41:8; James 2:23).

The New Testament reflects on this story by pointing out that Abraham was not deterred from believing God's promise of a son despite "his own body, already dead (since he was about a hundred years old), and the deadness of Sarah's womb" (Rom. 4:19). God likes to bring life from the dead! He gives hope beyond all hope.

And so, Abraham and Sarah gave birth to Isaac. Isaac and Rebekah gave birth to Jacob. From Jacob, Rachel, Leah, and their surrogates came the twelve tribes of Israel, from whom the Messiah was descended. The fact that the Jewish people exist to this very day, despite the Hamans, Herods, Hitlers, and more recently Hamas who have tried to destroy us, offers some of the most compelling evidence that God is real and that he keeps his promises.

God's promises don't stand because of how great Abraham's descendants are. In fact, the Bible shows how often we've been a great example of failure—just like the very nations from whom God set us apart. But God said, "I'm going to work with you. I'm going to do something extraordinary with you."

The Mystery of Being Chosen

Why did God stake his own reputation on the perpetuity of a particular Jewish family and the resulting nation of Israel? The Bible doesn't give an in-depth answer, but in Deuteronomy 7:7–8 we read, "The LORD did not set His love on you nor choose you because you were more in number than any other people, for you were the least of all peoples; but because the LORD loves you, and because He would keep the oath which He swore to your fathers." It seems that God simply wanted to show his covenant love and his power.

When you're Jewish it can be especially perplexing to hear that we are part of the chosen people, not only because we have been singled out so often for persecution, but also because identifying as God's chosen people can seem arrogant and exclusive. In fact, it would be exactly that—if not for the third part of God's promise to Abraham and Sarah.

God chose the Jewish people and made a covenant with us in order to bless all people, and the greatest fulfillment of that blessing is the Messiah. It's the Messiah who redeems humanity by addressing the fatal flaw that keeps us in doubt and distrust of God's love for us. How the Messiah does that is a subject of other prophecies. Here we rest our focus on that fact that God promises a blessing so great that it can't be contained in one person, family, or nation, but it bubbles up and flows to all the nations of the world.

What Jesus Said About Abraham

When Yeshua was discussing his messianic claims, he referred to this promise and told the Jewish leaders of his day, "Your father Abraham rejoiced that he would see my day. He saw it and was glad" (John 8:56 ESV). Jesus knew that he was fulfilling the promise that the Messiah would be the descendant of Abraham, through whom all nations would be blessed. He wanted the Jewish people to rejoice along with Abraham. He still does.

God continued to make promises and predictions about the coming Messiah throughout the Hebrew Scriptures. And yet those promises were often fulfilled in the strangest and most unexpected ways. Which is why, even when Jesus returned from the dead and was standing in the midst of his disciples, they needed him to open their minds and hearts to the greatest and most amazing blessing of all time.

AND YOU?

Whatever your ancestry, your family heritage likely contains much that is admirable, and some that is not. That's part of the human condition—being made in God's image and yet struggling against his boundaries. But if we believe God and open our minds to his plans, he is perfectly capable of blessing us and making us a blessing to others.

When you think about the blessings you would want for yourself and your family going forward, what does that look like? Have you considered that a God-given destiny starts and ends with his desire for all people to be blessed with the gift of his love and redemption?

"The scepter will not depart from Judah,
Nor the ruler's staff from between his feet,
Until Shiloh comes,
And to him shall be the obedience of the peoples."

Genesis 49:10 NASB

Messiah would be from the tribe of Judah.

CHAPTER 3

Member of the Tribe

One of my favorite Yiddish words is *beshert*. It expresses joy over something that was "meant to be."

Often people say "it was beshert" when explaining how they met the love of their life—or even to describe the actual person—"my beshert, my intended." In the midst of problems or mundane details, we might not see how "destiny" is putting us in just the right place at just the right time to receive something or someone wonderful. It's often only in hindsight that we recognize what was actually beshert. When Yeshua spent time reviewing messianic prophecies with his followers, he was opening their minds to his destiny and theirs.

The Pattern of Divine Destiny

All the messianic prophecies point to divine destiny. They reveal situations, circumstances, and not least of all, specific families and individuals through which the Messiah would come. It's not difficult to detect patterns in these prophecies. As we've begun to see, God makes messianic promises in dark and painful circumstances, and those promises are often counterintuitive, and sometimes even appear paradoxical.

"The seed of the woman" was at the very least a countercultural concept, if not a literal impossibility. And yet that was the first prediction of Messiah. Pay attention to the seed of the woman. Look to see what's coming from her, because God has chosen her offspring to deal with the source of evil in the world.

Generations later the Bible begins to narrow down that seed of the woman with Abraham and Sarah. From their lineage is coming a ray of hope that will bless all the nations. How counterintuitive was that? Sarah was so certain of her utter inability to conceive that she arranged a surrogate pregnancy between Abraham and Hagar—yet eventually she did give birth just as God had promised. And so, God's promise to Abraham and Sarah is passed to Isaac and Rebekah.

When Rebekah was pregnant with twin boys, God pronounced the blessing and authority on the younger brother (Jacob), though it normally would have been conferred on Esau as the firstborn (Gen. 25:23–25). Once again, God's choice is unexpected.

And now the revelation of divine destiny was further clarified as Jacob called his sons from his death bed: "Gather yourselves together, that I may tell you what shall happen to you in days to come" (Gen. 49:1 ESV).

Jacob's Deathbed Prophecy

Once again, it was a dark time as the light of the whole Jewish community, the last of the three epic patriarchs, was fading. His family was far from home, having been driven to Egypt through famine. Pharaoh treated them kindly for the sake of their brother Joseph, but the siblings couldn't help but wonder if Joseph would behave differently toward them once their father was gone. After all, they had sold him into slavery!

We don't know whether Abraham had passed down the prediction that his descendants would themselves endure four hundred years of slavery in Egypt (Gen. 15:13–16). We do know that with or without that knowledge, Jacob's impending death made life painful and uncertain for the tribes of Israel.

Against that backdrop, Jacob gave voice to this prophecy, providing another piece of the picture of the Messiah. He's going to come from a royal line, descended from the tribe of Judah. Judah is the one who will hold the scepter, the ruler's staff. If you are looking for the Messiah, keep your eyes on the tribe of Judah.

Once again, a ray of light shines in the darkness. From one of these brothers, a ruler or series of rulers is coming. Surely that rule implies power and authority to reverse life's harsh realities—displacement, alienation, and enslavement. The scepter shall not depart from Judah.

Why Judah?

Again, it's countercultural, counterintuitive. Judah isn't Jacob's oldest son, nor his favorite. He is the fourth son of Jacob and Leah. You may recall that from the first moment Jacob saw Rachel, he considered her his "beshert"—but he was tricked into marrying Leah, her older sister, first. As disappointing and upsetting as this deception was for Jacob, it was humiliating for Leah. She could never forget that she was not chosen, not wanted. But God showed Leah compassion by blessing her with children, while Rachel did not conceive for many years.

The first three times Leah gave birth, she chose names for her sons that reflected hope that she and Jacob would bond over their children, and he would grow to love her. But by her fourth pregnancy, Leah seemed to accept that Jacob would never feel toward her what he felt toward Rachel. And instead of looking to him for fulfillment, she now gave praise to God for *his* care. Accordingly, she named her fourth son Judah, which means praise.

We don't know for certain why God chose Judah as the tribe from which Messiah would come. But we can see that God's choices often differ significantly from people's natural inclinations or preferences.

So, Jacob was not establishing his own preferences when he gathered his sons to hear about their futures. He was reporting news of a destiny that God carefully planned and was revealing bit by bit.

Given God's pattern, it is not surprising that the prophecy concerning Judah is not only counterintuitive, but also contains an enigma.

The Mystery of Shiloh

The scepter will not depart from Judah, "until Shiloh comes" (Gen. 49:10). What does that mean?

Shiloh is a place in Israel where the tabernacle (the precursor to the temple) was housed during the time of the Judges. But is the prophecy talking about that location? It's unclear.

Some have rendered the word *Shiloh* as "tribute." But what would that tribute be, and to whom would it be paid?

Others understand the word *Shiloh* not as the place, but as a title for the one who will ultimately receive the scepter, that is, "the one to whom it belongs." Rabbinic interpretation often identifies that one as the Messiah.[1]

It makes sense that the ruler, King Messiah, would receive tribute. And from that standpoint, if Jesus is the Messiah as he claimed to be, the New Testament provides a plausible answer to the question of Shiloh.

Tribute to a Baby

The first four books of the New Testament are the life stories of Jesus, written by his disciples. They are known as the Gospels of Matthew, Mark, Luke, and John. Matthew and Luke make it clear that Jesus is descended from the tribe of Judah, but while the accounts overlap, each provides unique content about Jesus.

For example, we read in the gospel of Matthew that while Yeshua was still a baby, "wise men" from the east paid him a startling visit. "And going into the house, they saw the child with Mary his mother, and they fell down and worshiped him. Then, opening their treasures, they offered him gifts, gold and frankincense and myrrh" (Matt. 2:11 ESV).

We do not know how they knew about him, other than they had "seen His star" (Matt. 2:2) and were obviously expecting that the birth of a ruler of epic proportions would be revealed in the heavens. Clearly their actions and gifts were a tribute fit for royalty—and not just an ordinary tribal king. This worship, these treasures, only make sense if they were offered to a powerful ruler.

Yet these men did not journey to a palace where you would expect to find such a king, but to a simple, obscure house. Nor did they present their gifts to appease or win the protection of a warrior king. They paid tribute to a vulnerable child whose people were under the thumb of the Roman empire.

Tradition suggests that these "wise men" were kings from Arabia, Persia, and India. That speculation certainly fits well with the last phrase of the Genesis 49 prophecy: "to Him shall be the obedience of the people" (v. 10). The plural here indicates that it is not only Jewish people who will obey this king. Some translations render "the peoples" as "the nations."

This is consistent with God's promise that Abraham and Sarah's descendants would be a blessing to the nations. But how unexpected and seemingly paradoxical it is that the first rulers to pay tribute to Messiah were not from Israel, but from other nations.

World religions tend to be centered in either the West or in the East, and are strongly identified with specific people or ethnicities. But this event in the life of Jesus, depicted by so many Christians every year at Christmas, reminds us of what the Jewish Bible says about the Messiah. While he is a descendant of Israel and the Jewish people, the Messiah is the hope, the promise of a bright destiny for all people who will receive his light.

A Glimpse of Things to Come

Followers of Jesus come from just about every race and ethnicity on the planet. It may seem ironic that such a small minority of those followers are Jewish. And yet, it is no coincidence that the last book of the New Testament refers to Jesus as "the Lion of the tribe of Judah" (Rev. 5:5 ESV).

That book, which predicts how things will unfold at the end of time, refers to the role of the Jewish people and the Jewish Messiah . . . while also providing a sweeping look at the destiny of all humanity.

Other books in the New Testament predict a time when all Israel will recognize Yeshua as the Messiah. I believe that day will come, but until then, I know that faith in Jesus strikes many or even most of my people as paradoxical and problematic. That is why it's so important to consider the pattern in these prophecies . . . which are nearly always paradoxical and often, by human standards, problematic. The Creator of the universe is at work, often unseen, bringing about his ultimate purposes in strange and unexpected ways. But why should that surprise us? If God has more wisdom, more power, more patience than we do, why would he confine his plans to fit into our limited understanding and expectations? We can take comfort in the fact that God is able to work in seemingly impossible situations, and his promises are not contingent on how faithful we are, but how faithful he is.

One of the most beautiful promises that God made to Israel came in the midst of her captivity in Babylon in the sixth century BC (which had been predicted through the Jewish prophets as a consequence of disbelief and disobedience): "For I know the plans I have for you, declares the LORD, plans for welfare and not for evil, to give you a future and a hope" (Jer. 29:11 ESV).

That verse has been quoted and cherished by non-Jews who also hold these Scriptures to be sacred. And I believe that through Jesus, the Jewish Messiah, God extends this promise (which is still in effect to Israel) to people of all ethnicities.

AND YOU?

Do you think it is possible that God has a purpose and a plan for you? If so, what if the destiny God has for you is counterintuitive? Do you think God might see value and promise in people or things or ideas that you would tend to overlook? What would it take for you to ask him to open your mind to the plans he might have for you?

"The Lord your God will raise up for you a prophet like me from among you, from your brothers—it is to him you shall listen. . . . And I will put my words in his mouth, and he shall speak to them all that I command him. And whoever will not listen to my words that he shall speak in my name, I myself will require it of him."'

Deut. 18:15, 18–19 ESV

Messiah would be a prophet like Moses.

CHAPTER 4

Holy Moses

The young man shook his head and waved away the gospel pamphlet I was offering. "You Christians have Jesus. We Jews have Moses."

I knew this Arizona State University student was not interested in Jesus, but I was enjoying the sunshine and the fact that Lev had stopped to talk. His *yarmulke* or *kippah,* his small head covering, indicated that he was among the more religious Jewish students on campus.

I'd heard his remark many times. Lev was drawing a line between our beliefs—asserting that he and I followed two very different religions. And his implication was, as Rudyard Kipling wrote in his famous poem, *The Ballad of East and West,* "never the twain shall meet."

"What if I told you I have Moses *and* Jesus?" I replied. He was curious, so I quoted the messianic prophecy from Deuteronomy 18:15–19.

Lev listened as I pointed out that *Moshe Rabbeinu* (Hebrew for "Moses our teacher") had written about a future prophet to whom all of Israel would be answerable. Then I told him a little about Yeshua: how he faithfully followed the Law of Moses. How he wasn't interested in starting a new religion. How he came to fulfill God's promises to Israel and the nations.

We had a great conversation. Lev seemed glad to know that believers in Jesus hold Moses in high regard. He was not interested in the gospel at that point but could see that following Moses does not necessarily close the door to Jesus, or vice versa.

Yeshua himself was well-versed in the Hebrew Scriptures. That is why he told his opponents, "If you believed Moses, you would believe me" (John 5:46). I can only imagine how astonished Jesus' disciples must have been to realize the one of whom Deuteronomy 18 spoke was standing before them.

What Would It Take to Be a Prophet Like Moses?

The book of Deuteronomy concludes by telling us there was never a prophet like Moses, yet Moses promised there would be. So, what distinctives would a prophet need in order to fit that bill?

Role of redeemer: Moses is the one God chose to deliver Israel from slavery in Egypt. Next to God, Moses is the key player in the story of redemption—a story without which our people would not exist.

Relationship with God: The Scriptures also highlight Moses' unique relationship with God. "But since then there has not arisen in Israel a prophet like Moses, whom the LORD knew face to face" (Deut. 34:10). Other prophets hear the word of the Lord in dreams and visions, but Moses speaks to and hears from God directly.

Reflector of God's glory: Moses' face literally shines after his encounters with the Holy One. The people of Israel are so frightened by this reflection of God's glory that Moses wears a veil over his face after his meetings with God. (See Ex. 34:29–35.) The people simply are not ready to see the *kavod*—the glorious bright light of the Lord—shining from Moses.

Intercessor: Moses intercedes with God on behalf of Israel since the people are not only fearful of *seeing* God's glory, but tremble at the idea of *hearing* from God directly (Ex. 20:19). They beg Moses to be their "go-between," which is what God had intended anyway. Moses intercedes faithfully as he leads Israel through the wilderness for forty years. Not only does he pass on God's words to the people, but Moses speaks to God on their behalf when the people go astray (Ex. 32:30–33).

Miracle worker: A few prophets like Elijah and Elisha are remembered for their miracles, but none compares to Moses for the sheer number or overall impact of miracles, from turning the water in Egypt to blood, to the parting of the Red Sea, to obtaining water from a rock, to name a few.

Moses' Concern for the People

When Moses is about 120 years old, God tells him the second time to bring forth water from a rock—specifically, by speaking to it. However, Moses takes it upon himself to speak impatiently to the people and instead of speaking to the rock, he strikes it twice to drive his point home. As a result, God prohibits Moses from entering the promised land, though he does bring him up on a mountain to get a good look at it.

After God pronounces judgment, we see Moses' impatience with the people quickly turns to concern.

Moses knows they are fearful, and he speaks to God about it. What will they do now that their leader, the one who brought the nation out of slavery and to the very edge of the promised land—is about to die?

It appears Moses has heard the people wondering aloud *What's going to happen when Moses is gone? Who's going to talk to God for us?* They need a word of hope, a promise that someone else will lead and intercede with the same strength and power and with the same results.

God replies to Moses in Deuteronomy 18:17, "They are right in what they have spoken" (ESV). In other words, the people *do* need a prophet to intercede; they would not be able to handle God speaking directly to them. And then God makes the promise: "I will raise up for them a prophet like you from among their brothers. And I will put my words in his mouth, and he shall speak to them all that I command him. And whoever will not listen to my words that he shall speak in my name, I myself will require it of him" (vv. 18–19).

The book of Deuteronomy (in Hebrew *Devarim,* meaning "words") not only describes this coming prophet, but reaffirms the word of promise, the covenant that God had made with Israel. It assures the people that while Moses is not going with them into the promised land, they will not be alone.

Deuteronomy concludes by telling us there was never a prophet like Moses, and yet God promises to raise one up. It seems that promise was taking a long view—because as fine a leader as Joshua was, he was not "a prophet like Moses." Nor do any of the major or minor prophets in the Hebrew Scriptures fit that description. Yet we can see that promise fulfilled in Yeshua.

Yeshua and Moses: Alike, Yet Different

Moses was appointed to redeem the Jewish people from bondage to Pharaoh so that we could be free to love and serve God. Jesus also came to redeem the Jewish people, but his mission extended much further. He came to redeem people from every nation from the spiritual bondage that prevents us from truly loving and serving God. We all need to be set free from our persistent and self-destructive efforts to replace God's will and God's ways with our own.

Moses delivered God's law to set people apart for God, and for life according to his standards. Jesus did not dismiss the law, but took it deeper, emphasizing the spirit of the law as a guide to living.

It's good to have external standards to help us live as God desires, but we all fall short of those standards. That is why grace and truth came through *Yeshua Ha Mashiach*, Jesus the Messiah (John 1:17). Through Jesus, we can know from within how God wants us to live. (This was also prophesied in the Jewish Bible and will be unpacked in section 2.) Because of what Messiah did to redeem us (see chapter 7), we can receive God's grace and forgiveness.

Moses' encounters with God showed on his countenance; it shone supernaturally when he came down from the mountain because God had spoken to him "face to face" (See Ex. 33:11 and Ex. 34:29–34.) Like Moses, Jesus didn't need a vision to hear from or to speak for God; and his countenance reflected his direct encounters with the Father. In Matthew's gospel, we see how Jesus took two of his closest disciples with him onto a mountain, where they saw him much as Moses must have appeared to the people of Israel. Unlike Moses though, it was not only Jesus' face that shone, but also "His clothes became as white as the light" (Matt. 17:2). And the disciples saw, standing there with Yeshua, none other than Moses and Elijah! Then from a bright cloud came a voice, "This is My beloved Son, in whom I am well pleased. Hear Him!" (Matt. 17:5).

Moses was known for his miracles, as mentioned earlier in this chapter, and Jesus was also known to perform many miracles. When Jesus spoke, blind people were able to see, and those who were lame could walk. One boy's meager lunch could feed five thousand people. People who were tormented by demons, both literally and figuratively, were set free. The dead were raised back to life. (See, for example, Matt. 9:27–31; 14:15–21; Mark 1:23–28; Luke 7:11–18; John 5:1–9; 6:9–13.)

Making the Connection Between Moses and Jesus

Multitudes of Jewish people who saw the miracles Yeshua performed made the connection: "When the people saw the sign that he had done, they said, 'This is indeed the Prophet who is to come into the world!'" (John 6:14 ESV). They were looking for the prophet Moses had promised, and here he was!

Peter confirmed that when he spoke to a large crowd of Jewish pilgrims who'd come to Jerusalem for the Festival of Shavuot (Pentecost). In his sermon about Jesus, he reminded them: "Moses said, 'The Lord God will raise up for you a prophet like me [Moses] from your brothers. You shall listen to him in whatever he tells you'" (Acts 3:22 ESV).

Later in the New Testament (in the book of Hebrews) we read that not only is Yeshua like Moses, but he is greater than Moses. As significant as Moses is and always will be in the history of the Jewish people, in the context of God's plan to redeem humanity, Moses provided a picture and foreshadowing of what Messiah Yeshua would be and do.

More and more Jewish people are finding that Yeshua is that prophet like Moses, the ray of light in the darkness who will take all his followers—Jewish or Gentile—to the ultimate promised land, the very presence of God.

At the beginning of this chapter, I recalled a conversation with a student who thought that people had to choose between Moses and Jesus, and that the Jewish choice would have to be Moses. I included a familiar quote from a Kipling poem about East and West that says "never the twain shall meet." But did you know that by quoting it out of context, as people often do, we lose the true meaning of the poem? Ironically, Kipling's poem is not about mutually exclusive views at all. Rather, it challenges readers to consider that regardless of people's differences, they have more in common than meets the eye. Context matters. Without it, it's easy to lose the author's intent.

AND YOU?

Do you tend to see Moses and Jesus as leaders of mutually exclusive religions? If so, I hope the clues about the Jewish Messiah that we've explored in these four chapters have encouraged you to keep digging into the biblical context as you explore matters of faith.

That biblical context can assure us that if we follow Yeshua, we are not only following Moses, but all the prophets. And it is to those prophets we now turn.

Clues About Messiah in the Prophets

The prophets of the Bible were the conscience of ancient Israel as they spoke God's message to the people. They called the people of their day—including their leaders—to repent from sin. In this way, they held people accountable to obey God. They also spoke of events yet to come, offering visions of judgment for sin, as well as restoration to a glorious future. All these aspects of prophecy coalesced in their visions of an individual—later called the Messiah—who would redeem Israel by himself taking on the burden of the nation's sins.

In this section we will look at four passages from the prophets. Isaiah 7 offers hope in dark times through the promise of a messianic child yet to be born, while Micah 5 speaks about Messiah's birthplace. Isaiah chapter 53 presents one of the most remarkable portraits of Messiah, including specific details of his mission to bring redemption. Finally, Jeremiah describes the messianic future in terms of a "new covenant." The promises first articulated in the Torah find a rich development in the words of the biblical prophets.

"Therefore the Lord Himself will give you a sign: Behold, the virgin shall conceive and bear a Son, and shall call His name Immanuel."

Isaiah 7:14

Messiah would be born of a virgin.

CHAPTER 5

What's the Hardest Miracle to Believe?

Years ago, talk show host Larry King invited me, along with a Baptist theologian, to debate two Orthodox rabbis live on CNN. The topic was whether or not Jesus is the Jewish Messiah.

I arrived at the studio early and had some time with Larry King before the show.

What a Famous Talk Show Host Would Ask Jesus

Mr. King, who was Jewish, confided in me, "Of all the people in all of history that I would love to interview, my number one choice would be Jesus of Nazareth. My first question would be, 'Were you really born of a virgin?'"

I hadn't expected that. "Why would that be your first question, Larry?"

He answered, "Come on! Seriously? Who could really believe something like that?"

I responded, "It *is* amazing, but don't you think the God who called this whole universe into existence could also suspend the laws of nature and make it possible for a virgin to conceive and have a son?"

We discussed it for a few minutes, and then I quoted from Isaiah to point out that with God, not only was this possible but it was inevitable—because God had said that it would happen.

We were running out of time before the show, and Larry concluded, "Well, it seems preposterous to me. How can you ever really know?"

I said, "Larry, the Bible says, 'You will seek Me and find Me, when you search for Me with all your heart. I will be found by you, says the LORD'" (Jer. 29:13–14).

Larry responded, "Yes, but who wrote that?"

I answered, "A nice Jewish boy named Jeremiah wrote that." And for a moment that most skilled and talkative of interviewers grew silent and pondered. It was a moment I will never forget.

I found it intriguing that this miracle was at the top of the list of questions that Larry King most wanted to ask Jesus. But then, whenever Isaiah 7:14 is mentioned in regard to Jesus, it becomes a topic of hot debate. Is it or isn't it a messianic prophecy? Does it or does it not really speak of a son conceived by a virgin?

Many people, rabbis included, simply dismiss the idea as impossible based on the laws of nature. But one might as well say that there is no such thing as miracles—because why should one miracle be any more impossible (or possible) than another? And as I pointed out to Mr. King, if God is real, he created the laws of nature and can certainly control or even overrule them. The more logical dispute concerns the meaning and intention of the Isaiah 7:14 text.

The Controversy over the Hebrew Word for Virgin

The Hebrew word that many translate as "virgin" in Isaiah 7:14 is *almah*. Actually, *almah* does not literally mean *virgin*. It means "young woman of marriageable age."

Another Hebrew word that some say is more likely to be translated virgin is *betulah*. Many have argued that if Isaiah really meant to predict a virgin giving birth, he would have used the word *betulah*.

However, the word *betulah* is not used exclusively to mean virgin. For example, in Joel 1:8 a young woman, *betulah*, is lamenting the death of her husband.

So neither word, *almah* nor *betulah,* would conclusively prove that Isaiah was speaking of a virgin. Why did Isaiah choose the word *almah* in this passage rather than *betulah*? I don't know. Either word could have been used to mean virgin, and either could be disputed. I do know that well before Jesus was born, an eminent group of Jewish translators believed that Isaiah was speaking of a virgin.

The Controversy Resolved

Long before the Hebrew Scriptures were available in English, they were translated into Greek. That Greek translation is called the Septuagint and, according to tradition, seventy Jewish scholars (some say seventy-two) in Alexandria, Egypt, completed the translation around the third to first centuries BC.

When those scholars translated the word *almah* from Isaiah 7:14 into Greek, they used the word *parthenos*, which specifically means a virgin. The Hebrew translators at that time clearly believed that the prophet Isaiah was referring to a virgin. We can see why by looking at the context of the culture, the context of the verse, and the context of the promise of a Messiah.

The cultural context: In the time and place that Isaiah wrote, young women were presumed to be virgins until they married.

The textual content: Isaiah announced this birth as a clear and direct work of God: "The Lord himself will give you a sign . . ." When a young woman gives birth to a child, that isn't much of a sign, is it? Given the cultural and textual context, the translators of the Septuagint made an unambiguous choice; they used the word *parthenos* to indicate that this young woman would somehow conceive without the agency of sexual intercourse. The resulting birth is an extraordinary sign.

The context of the messianic hope: Remember that the very first prophecy concerning the coming of the Messiah dates all the way back to the earliest time in human history. This prophecy is built upon the earliest of predictions, unpacked in chapter 1 of this book. Moses wrote in Genesis 3 that the head of the serpent would be crushed by the seed of the woman. The seed of the woman announced there is traditionally understood to be the Messiah.

To quickly review, the idea of "the seed of the woman" is found nowhere else in Scripture. When discussing offspring, the Bible and other literature of antiquity normally refer to the seed of the man. But what Genesis 3 hinted at is now revealed in Isaiah 7:14. A woman, in fact a virgin, would give birth to the Messiah without the agency of a man. Talk about miraculous!

So, if the scholars who translated the Hebrew Scriptures into Greek believed that Isaiah was speaking of a virgin, what changed? The sign God gave was not quite what (or who) those who came later were expecting.

This prophecy was fulfilled by Yeshua seven hundred years later according to the authors of the New Testament, beginning with Matthew and Luke. Clearly, Luke had interviewed Yeshua's mother, Miriam (Mary), and gave a personal account from her perspective (see Luke 1:26–35). Matthew, on the other hand, tells it from Joseph's perspective.

Dealing with the Unexpected

Joseph was betrothed to Miriam when he learned about her pregnancy. He had decided to quietly break the engagement, but changed his mind and chose to go through with the marriage. He had one reason and one reason only—but it was compelling. An angel of the Lord revealed to Joseph that Miriam's pregnancy was a direct fulfillment of Isaiah's prophecy: "All this took place to fulfill what the Lord had spoken by the prophet: 'Behold, the virgin shall conceive and bear a son, and they shall call his name Immanuel' (which means, God with us)" (Matt. 1:22–23 ESV).

It's significant that this and other prophecies tell of Messiah's birth and early life. Usually when people think of the Messiah, it's in his full-grown messianic role: a modern-day biblical hero, a great military leader. And some of the prophecies certainly describe him as such. But Isaiah is telling us that a child is to be born. And then we see Miriam and Joseph having to contend with a vulnerable baby, whose very birth made them vulnerable as well.

Throughout his mission, Yeshua fulfilled one prophecy after another, but even so, he was not what people were expecting. Many Jewish people gladly received him, but many of the religious authorities did not. I think that had some bearing on why later interpretations of the Isaiah 7 passage have steered away from the idea of a virgin.

Once again, we are reminded of seeming problems and paradoxes that characterize so many of the messianic promises and predictions. But bit by bit, these details come together to paint a picture of God's epic plan to restore human beings to the peace and joy we were meant to experience with him. The name Isaiah gives in this passage speaks to that very plan: the virgin who gives birth to a son will call him "Immanuel," which is Hebrew for "God is with us."

Multiple Names for Messiah?

Some have assumed that since Miriam named her baby Yeshua and not Immanuel, he cannot be the fulfillment of Isaiah 7:14. But while Immanuel was not his actual name, it was a description of who he is.

It's not unusual for people to have more than one name in the Bible. For example, the Scriptures say that one of King David's sons should be called "Jedidiah" because the Lord loves him (2 Sam. 12:25). *Jedidiah* is Hebrew for "beloved of God," but most people know this particular son of David by a different name: Solomon.

In biblical Jewish tradition, certain people received a second name to describe their character or destiny. The name that Miriam and Joseph were told to give the child was Yeshua, which is a combination of the Hebrew name of God and the word for "deliver" or "save." Isaiah 7 gives us another name for Yeshua, promising that the God who saves actually comes to dwell with us, to be in our midst.

Immanuel is not the only amazing name Isaiah gives for the Messiah, nor is it the only time he connects such names to the birth of a child. In Isaiah 9:6 we read: "For unto us a Child is born, unto us a Son is given; and the government will be upon his shoulder. And his name will be called Wonderful, Counselor, Mighty God, Everlasting Father, Prince of Peace."

Isaiah is contending that the Messiah would be more than an ordinary human being. He would be supernatural, by virtue of his virgin birth and by virtue of his nature, being "God with us." God chose a way to be with us that no ordinary person could choose. Astounding? Yes. Preposterous? Not if there truly is a God in heaven who cares to have a real relationship with us.

I've often thought back to my time with Larry King. I was glad to know that he'd thought about questions he would have for Jesus. I have a feeling that if he could have gone back in time to look into the eyes of Yeshua, his questions might have taken a different turn.

AND YOU?

Do you believe God can perform miracles? If you do, the virgin birth probably isn't as big of a question for you as it was for Larry King. Is there anything else that you would want to ask Jesus? If he is who so many believe him to be, it's not necessary to go back in time to ask him questions. I'm not saying you will hear an audible answer, but I believe that he wants to hear from you and will make it clear to you. If Jesus is truly *Immanuel,* maybe the question is not so much how God came to be with us, but why.

That question is answered in another of Isaiah's prophecies—chapter 53, where you'll find the most dramatic and extensive portrait of the Messiah in all of the Hebrew Bible.

But you, O Bethlehem Ephrathah, who are too little to be among the clans of Judah, from you shall come forth for me one who is to be ruler in Israel, whose coming forth is from of old, from ancient days.

Micah 5:2 ESV; 5:1 in the Hebrew Bible

Messiah would be born in Bethlehem, from the royal line of King David.

CHAPTER 6

A Big Deal over a Little Town

Bethlehem is only about five miles from Jerusalem, yet they are worlds apart. As you may know, Bethlehem today is an exclusively Arab town, part of the Palestinian territories. Israeli buses and tour guides are not permitted to cross to or from the territories.

There are many good Arab tour guides in Bethlehem, but chances are you won't see Jewish tourists lining up to see the Church of the Nativity, the shepherds' fields, or the olive wood shops. Christian tourists, on the other hand, might not even notice the lack of Jewish atmosphere around the birthplace of Jesus.

This strikes me as a strange present-day reality—paradoxical even. And there is more than one paradox concerning Bethlehem. For anyone who might still be expecting the Jewish Messiah to come, it's worth noting that he would not be able to fulfill Micah's prophecy about his birthplace today.

Of course, the "little town of Bethlehem" referred to in the well-known Christmas carol was once a very Jewish place. In fact, Bethlehem in Hebrew is *Beit Lechem*, which means "House of Bread." It was the birthplace of King David. Jerusalem is known as the City of David because he ruled from there. Yet in the gospel of Luke, it is Bethlehem—Yeshua's birthplace—that is referred to as the City of David (Luke 2:4).

A Jewish Woman's Christmas Carol Experience

Although the song "O Little Town of Bethlehem" may seem like it has little or nothing to do with the Jewish Messiah today, it's a different story for those who know about the history of the place and the promise of the Messiah. In fact, it's a story that captured the heart of a nineteen-year-old woman as she was rediscovering her Jewish identity.

She'd been raised by seriously Orthodox parents and graduated from Hebrew school at age twelve, at which point she questioned her upbringing and her faith in God. She married her high school sweetheart at eighteen. He, while also Jewish, had been raised more nominally Orthodox. He knew his wife liked Christmas carols—not for any spiritual reasons, but simply for the pleasure of the music. So he bought her a couple of record albums, collections of carols. He never dreamed that hearing "O Little Town of Bethlehem" might be the start of a new chapter in her life—and his.

In fact, the words brought back a fleeting memory of another carol that she'd sung in her high school chorus: "O Come, O Come, Emmanuel."[1] At the time, it had occurred to her that this Christmas song was saying that Jesus had come for her people, the Jewish people. And it seemed so paradoxical that Gentiles would believe in Jesus, and call him Emmanuel, which is Hebrew for "God with us," while she was forbidden to say his name. But she quickly shrugged it off.

Now, three years later, the carol "O Little Town of Bethlehem" brought back thoughts about Jesus and why she was not supposed to believe in him, but this time she could not shrug it off. As a new wife and mother, she was deeply grateful to God. She wanted to know him and raise her child to know him.

She wondered about the lyrics, "The hopes and fears of all the years are met in thee tonight." Did the hopes refer to the Messiah? She knew the Gentiles believed that. Did she fear thinking about Jesus because it might be true?

She resolved to ask God to show her the truth, and promised to follow him if he showed her that she should go back to Orthodox Judaism. Likewise, she promised to follow him if it meant believing in Jesus as the promised Messiah.

Within a year, Ceil Rosen came to believe that Jesus truly is the Jewish Messiah. So did her husband Moishe, who later became the founder of Jews for Jesus. Moishe was a mentor to me, and he taught me a great deal, but more importantly he encouraged me to continually study and learn from the Bible for myself. And while I've often thought and written about Micah's prediction of Messiah's birthplace over the years, more recently I've been impressed with the context in which it was written.

Another Promise to Pierce the Darkness

Micah wrote in approximately 700 B.C. In the verse preceding the prophecy, he says, "Siege is laid against us; with a rod they strike the judge of Israel on the cheek" (Micah 5:1 ESV; 4:14 in the Hebrew Bible). That verse refers to King Sennacharib and the Assyrians, who had invaded and laid siege to the city of Jerusalem.

King Hezekiah and Jerusalem were in serious trouble, but Micah pointed out that just five miles down the road, Bethlehem still stood as a beacon of hope. This was a timely reminder of an ancient prophecy that had yet to be fulfilled.

You see, three hundred years before Micah wrote these words, God made a promise to King David that the Messiah would come from his line, and that his throne and kingdom would endure forever (2 Samuel 7). In fact, an ancient phrase that continues as a popular song among many Jewish people today is, "David Melech Yisrael, Chai chai v'kayom! David, King of Israel, lives forever."[2] Clearly David himself died at a ripe old age, yet somehow through his line, and through the Messiah, he would live and reign forever.

In the Jerusalem Talmud, Bethlehem is mentioned as the birthplace of the Messiah. In a strange conversation between a Jewish man and an Arab man, we find this exchange: "The King Messiah has been born." "Where is he from?" "From the royal city, Bethlehem in Judah."[3]

And that is exactly why this ray of hope comes from Micah in yet another dark time of Israel's history. Yes, David's throne in Jerusalem is being threatened by the Assyrians, yet the future rule of Messiah Son of David is as sure as ever.

An Ancient Baby?

Then Micah adds something astounding to our understanding of the Messiah in this prophecy. While the place of Messiah's birth is humble ("too little to be among the clans of Judah"), his origin, or "coming forth," is glorious: from of old, from ancient days. Here Micah uses two Hebrew words, *kedem* and *olam*, which mean "ancient times" and "eternity." This child to be born in Bethlehem is ancient. An ancient baby? From eternity?! Though the word *olam* by itself might not denote eternity, according to one scholar, "when *qedem* and *olam* are used together, however, as in Proverbs 8:22–23, they always denote eternity past (cf. Deut. 33:27). In Mic. 5:2, these words are placed together to emphasize the ruler's true origin, being far earlier than his arrival in Bethlehem or even antiquity. Rather, he comes from eternity past."[4]

What an amazing, startling, and yes, paradoxical claim. Remember that the Messiah is from the tribe of Judah. He is Jewish. He is from the royal line of David. And now we see that he is from Bethlehem—yet he somehow existed from eternity.

Some might say, "But wait, Jesus is from Nazareth, right?" Jesus grew up in Nazareth, but he was born in Bethlehem. We know from the New Testament accounts that a Roman census was imposed upon the people of Israel for the purpose of collecting taxes. Joseph was obliged to leave Nazareth and "report" to Bethlehem; naturally he would not want to leave Miriam (Mary's Jewish name) behind just as Yeshua was about to be born. Rome wanted its money, but God had bigger things in mind. The seven-hundred-year-old promise that Messiah, the descendant of David, would be born in Bethlehem converged with the Roman census, all in God's timing.

As a confirmation the birth of the Messiah was part of God's plan to bless the nations, he used a star to alert wise men from the East (Matthew 2). These people, traditionally believed to be kings and also known as Magi, go off to Jerusalem and innocently ask Herod where they can find "the one who was born King of the Jews." Herod, of course, assumes that his throne is in jeopardy and is determined to eliminate the threat. So, he asks the Jewish leaders and Torah experts where the Messiah is supposed to be born.

Without hesitation, they tell him the Messiah is to be born in Bethlehem. (Statements in ancient rabbinic literature corroborate that expectation.)[5] Herod then tells the Magi to look for the child in Bethlehem, and report back to him. As they head toward Bethlehem, the star guides them to Yeshua. But after these wise men pay homage to him in Bethlehem, God warns them in a dream that Herod is seeking his life, so they go home another way.

Satisfying the Hunger for God

And so that baby who was somehow ancient—who was born in an insignificant town, yet whose significance is from everlasting— grew. His name was Yeshua (Jesus) and when the time came to begin revealing his identity, he boldly claimed to have existed before he was born. (See John 8:58.) What's more, he called people to follow him in ways that no rabbi had ever dared suggest to his students. The one born in the little town that literally means "the house of bread" said that he was the Bread of Life and promised that whoever came to him would never be hungry again. (See John 6:35, 48.) He was not talking about physical hunger, but spiritual hunger.

Spiritual hunger may seem like an abstract concept, but one way to look at it is to consider the contrast between Herod and the Magi. The Magi eagerly followed the star God provided to alert them to the birth of the "King of the Jews." They were looking up, not only literally, but metaphorically, ready to receive word from God about something that he was doing. Herod, on the other hand, saw the birth of Messiah as a threat to his right to rule. He was not hungry for what God was doing; he was hungry to maintain his own power.

AND YOU?

What about you? What are you hungry for? Are you looking for the truth about Jesus—even if it means that he has a right to rule your life? All of us have a natural tendency to resist God's rule in our lives. The Bible goes so far as to call it rebellion against God—which is the very essence of sin. God is willing to overcome that sin if you want him to; that is why he promised the Messiah in the first place. How does the Messiah overcome sin? We'll explore that in the next chapter.

Behold, My Servant shall deal prudently;
He shall be exalted and extolled and be very high.
Just as many were astonished at you,
So His visage was marred more than any man,
And His form more than the sons of men;
So shall He sprinkle many nations.
Kings shall shut their mouths at Him;
For what had not been told them they shall see,
And what they had not heard they shall consider.

Who has believed our report?
And to whom has the arm of the LORD been revealed?
For He shall grow up before Him as a tender plant,
And as a root out of dry ground.
He has no form or comeliness;
And when we see Him,
There is no beauty that we should desire Him.
He is despised and rejected by men,
A Man of sorrows and acquainted with grief.
And we hid, as it were, our faces from Him;
He was despised, and we did not esteem Him.

Surely He has borne our griefs
And carried our sorrows;
Yet we esteemed Him stricken,
Smitten by God, and afflicted.
But He was wounded for our transgressions,
He was bruised for our iniquities;
The chastisement for our peace was upon Him,
And by His stripes we are healed.
All we like sheep have gone astray;
We have turned, every one, to his own way;
And the LORD has laid on Him the iniquity of us all.

He was oppressed and He was afflicted,
Yet He opened not His mouth;
He was led as a lamb to the slaughter,
And as a sheep before its shearers is silent,
So He opened not His mouth.
He was taken from prison and from judgment,
And who will declare His generation?
For He was cut off from the land of the living;
For the transgressions of My people He was stricken.
And they made His grave with the wicked—
But with the rich at His death,
Because He had done no violence,
Nor was any deceit in His mouth.

Yet it pleased the LORD to bruise Him;
He has put Him to grief.
When You make His soul an offering for sin,
He shall see His seed, He shall prolong His days,
And the pleasure of the LORD shall prosper in His hand.
He shall see the labor of His soul, and be satisfied.
By His knowledge My righteous Servant shall justify many,
For He shall bear their iniquities.
Therefore I will divide Him a portion with the great,
And He shall divide the spoil with the strong,
Because He poured out His soul unto death,
And He was numbered with the transgressors,
And He bore the sin of many,
And made intercession for the transgressors.

Isaiah 52:13–53:12

Messiah would suffer and die for the sin of his people.

CHAPTER 7

The Dilemma of the Missing Prophecy

Countless people have had their lives forever changed by a passage from the Hebrew Bible—one that is missing from the yearly synagogue readings. My colleague Avi Snyder told me a story of one such person, a Jewish woman named Miriam. What happened while he and another colleague, Julia, were visiting her has happened time and time again.

"Do you have a Bible?" Julia asked. Miriam nodded, quickly scanned her bookcase, and handed a copy of the Scriptures to Julia. "Let me show you something," Julia said. She opened the Bible to Isaiah, chapter 53, placed the Bible back into Miriam's hands, and asked her to read it out loud.

When Miriam finished reading this remarkable passage about a servant of the Lord who dies for the transgressions of his people, Julia asked, "Does this sound like anyone you've ever heard about?"

"It sounds like Jesus," Miriam said, very matter-of-factly.

"Do you know where you're reading from in the Bible?"

"From the New Testament," she said, with the confidence of someone stating the obvious.

Julia and Avi exchanged a quick smile. "Actually," Julia said, "you were reading from the Hebrew Scriptures, the Old Testament."

Miriam was startled. She read through the passage again, this time silently. Then she looked up and asked, "Why don't our rabbis believe this?"

"Actually, that's the wrong question," Julia answered with a sympathetic half-grin. "The *right* question is, 'Why don't *you* believe this?'"

Miriam stared at her Bible in her hands. She thought for a moment, then quietly said, "I do."

I have had so many similar experiences, reading these verses to Jewish friends—and then asking who they think the passage is describing. More often than not, the response is, "Of course that's Jesus, but you're reading from the New Testament."

Most are stunned to hear, "No, this is from the prophet Isaiah, straight out of the Jewish Bible. It was written seven hundred years before Jesus ever walked the earth."

How is it that most of us raised in Jewish homes have been so very unfamiliar with this passage from our own Bible? Our rabbis excised this portion from the haftarah reading cycle long ago, so it is never read aloud in the synagogue.[1] Why? Maybe a better question is, now that you've seen it, is your mind open to what it is saying?

Who Is the Servant?

To understand this unique passage, it helps to know that the book of Isaiah contains four servant passages also called "Servant Songs": Isaiah 42:1–4; Isaiah 49:1–6; Isaiah 50:4–11;

and Isaiah 52:13–53:12. In the first three passages, the servant is often referring to Israel—and many believe that Isaiah 53 refers to Israel as well. But this fourth servant song is different, and a close look shows it clearly is not about Israel.

As Hebrew scholar Dominick Hernández points out, "The inspired poet's crafty, polyvalent (i.e., having more than one meaning) servant language provokes us to perpetually wonder to whom or what the 'servant' might refer." Hernández notes that unlike the previous servant songs, Isaiah 53 introduces "the motif that the servant will suffer on behalf of the transgression of others, becomes the victim of divinely imposed distress for the sake of others to bring about peace for them. Thus, it is unlikely that the prophet is indicating the community or even a portion of the people will suffer on behalf of itself."[2]

Note that in order to bear the transgressions of others, the servant would have to be innocent of any wrongdoing himself.[3] No one, Jewish or otherwise, would claim that for Israel (or for any other person or people).

Then too, other passages from Isaiah refer to Israel as a beneficiary of the servant. For example, in Isaiah 49:6 (ESV), God says to the servant, "It is too light a thing that you should be my servant to raise up the tribes of Jacob and to bring back the preserved of Israel; I will make you as a light for the nations, that my salvation may reach to the end of the earth."

In other words, it is not enough that the servant is going to be speaking to his own people, but God will also make the servant a light to the nations so that God's salvation may reach to the end of the earth. That is definitely a messianic motif, and a reminder of Genesis 12:3, "In you all the families of the earth shall be blessed."

The idea that the suffering servant of Isaiah 53 refers to Israel was popularized by the great eleventh-century rabbi Rashi. Prior to that it would seem most scholarly Jewish sources considered the text to be speaking of the Messiah. Why did Rashi's argument gain so much traction when it was contrary to the majority opinion?

One could speculate that because Rashi was writing during the Crusades, which was a time of terrible persecution against the Jewish people, it might have been comforting to see the deaths of thousands of Jews as somehow meaningful. But that doesn't explain why so many people today accept Rashi's view without question. Could it be because it provides a sanctioned alternative for what many find an uncomfortable dilemma? If this passage is actually meant to be about the Jewish Messiah, why does it sound so much like Jesus? I've seen many people struggle with that dilemma. The most memorable was the reaction of an entire class of Jewish college students.

Decades ago, I studied at Spertus College of Judaica in Chicago. My studies included a twelve-week course on the book of Isaiah. Although we had sixty-six chapters to cover, we spent an entire class session on one chapter. In fact, the session was spent addressing a single question: who was Isaiah speaking of in chapter 53?

I can still picture those twenty eager Jewish students leaning forward with anticipation. Not one bored expression could be seen as the erudite professor (who happened to be a Christian) offered possible answers to the identity of this suffering servant, including the prophet Isaiah himself, the nation of Israel, the prophet Jeremiah, and finally the Messiah.

I listened as the students shot down each proposal. One after another they dismissed traditional Jewish interpretations until it came to the last one: the prophet was speaking of the Messiah. The tension, the angst in the room was palpable. The unspoken question hung in the air: *if this prophecy is about the Messiah, why does it sound so much like Jesus?* It seemed no one would dare to say his name or make the connection out loud, not even the professor.

The hour ended, and the students filed out, looking dissatisfied and even disappointed. Maybe they wanted more convincing proof that the text could not possibly be pointing to Jesus, or maybe they wanted to hear that they were not foolish for thinking it sounded like him, I don't know. I was there to learn and at that point did not initiate conversations about my beliefs or affiliation with Jews for Jesus. (Eventually it did come out.) In any case, Jesus was the proverbial elephant in the room, because nothing and no one else seemed to fit this perplexing passage.

An Unexpected Hero

And so, yet another prophecy reminds us that God is in the habit of doing things differently than we would expect. The Jewish people have long been waiting for a "hero-Messiah," the kind who would ride in on a white horse, vanquish evil rulers, bring justice, and basically solve all our problems.

To be fair, we had good reason to expect a conquering hero. The Hebrew Scriptures speak about the Messiah coming in the clouds of heaven with angels, talk about him winning the war to end all wars, and more . . . so why wouldn't people base their expectations on those passages? Why would we consider, much less expect, a Messiah who would suffer and die? Just one reason: God provided two seemingly conflicting pictures of what the Messiah would do. We don't have the liberty to dismiss one picture in favor of the other.

Traditional Judaism has suggested that God offers two Messiahs: Messiah ben David (the conquering king) and Messiah ben Joseph (who suffers and dies). According to the medieval Jewish philosopher Saadia Gaon, the former comes if we are faithfully keeping the Law, the latter if we are not.[4] But Yeshua opened his followers' minds to see how these prophetic pieces are painting a single portrait of the same Messiah.

Only God in his great wisdom could provide a series of prophecies that would shape our expectations of the Messiah, while still giving us what we never expected. And only in hindsight can we see how the role of the conquering King Messiah was actually predicated on his success as the suffering servant. There was a road Messiah had to walk in order to make his ultimate victory our victory as well. We can't truly understand our King Messiah, the Great Conqueror, until we know what it took for him to win.

Who knew that our hero would come to suffer and die? We naturally want heroes to sweep in and save us from desperate situations and circumstances beyond our control. But God wants to rescue us from so much more than that. He wants to save us from ourselves, and all the consequences of our sin—all the brokenness and delusions that alienate us from him. We can't expect that kind of salvation to ride in on a white horse. God's salvation goes far deeper and gets much more personal than that. My salvation (and yours) begins with a change of heart, not a change of government.

There's a Hebrew word for "my salvation" that appears in an earlier servant song in Isaiah 49: "*Yeshuati*." It is fitting, and certainly no coincidence, that Jesus' Hebrew name is Yeshua. He fulfilled the promise of the servant who was Israel's greatest son, the Messiah. And now Isaiah invites us to expect the unexpected as we look at the appearance, the agony, and the accomplishment of this servant who is our Messiah.

Messiah's Appearance, Agony, and Accomplishment

His physical features did not convey any greatness—in fact his appearance was "marred" (Isa. 52:14). "Who has believed our report?" the prophet asks in Isaiah 53:1. In other words, "Isn't this unbelievable?!" No outward appeal would cause us to want him, to follow him (Isaiah 53:2). Once again, God does the unexpected. Isaiah's prediction ultimately shocks and shatters our preconceptions of how God would save us.

We see the *agony* of the servant in Isaiah 53:3–8. His suffering is actually part of the plan of God. He was pierced for our transgressions. He was wounded. By his stripes (referring to the torn flesh caused by floggings) we are healed. Verse 6 is the key to understanding the reason for the servant's agony: "All we like sheep have gone astray; we have turned, every one, to his own way; and the LORD has laid on Him the iniquity of us all." This is the mission of Messiah that goes all the way back to Genesis 3. Before he conquers the obvious problems of the world, he deals with the brokenness of our hearts. The prophets not only tell us how Messiah would be born, and where he would be born, but this stunning prophecy is telling us *why* he would be born. Ultimately it is to bring about redemption, salvation, and restoration from the brokenness that afflicts us all.

Which brings us to the *accomplishment* of the servant. His agony would not be the end of the story, but the portal through which he would pass into triumph. Agony would lead to victory. Some translations say he will "see his offspring," but the Hebrew word for offspring here is *zera*, which means "seed." Either word could be taken metaphorically to mean this person lives to see the outcome, or the fruit, of what he's done.

He will prolong his days, Isaiah says. He then goes on to speak of all the things God will do with this servant "because he poured out his soul to death" (v. 12). How could the servant die, and then go on to do all these things? He will be raised from the dead. Through his resurrection, Jesus completed the work of redemption. That was his purpose. That was why he came.

81

Death Swallowed Up in Victory

Once again, imagine with me Jesus—having been crucified and buried—now standing before his disciples alive, opening their minds to how the Scriptures had predicted it all. This reality transformed their lives. First-century followers of Yeshua sang their own servant song about it:

> But [He] made Himself of no reputation, taking the form of a bondservant, and coming in the likeness of men. And being found in appearance as a man, He humbled Himself and became obedient to the point of death, even the death of the cross. Therefore God also has highly exalted Him and given Him the name which is above every name, that at the name of Jesus every knee should bow, of those in heaven, and of those on earth, and of those under the earth, and that every tongue should confess that Jesus Christ is Lord, to the glory of God the Father. (Phil. 2:7–11)

This song basically translated Isaiah 53 into the New Testament language of those early Jewish followers of Yeshua. Isaiah 53 had been fulfilled. Jesus lived a life that we could not live. He died the death that we, in our rebellion against God, all deserved. But Yeshua did not deserve to die; death could not hold him, and the grave could not keep him. He came back from the grave, and now that same resurrection power of God is available to all those who believe in the Messiah, the suffering servant, the resurrected Lord. We are his seed.

One day, the Messiah will return as the King who conquers all oppressors. But what good would that be to you, me, or anyone else if, in our hearts, we won't admit that we need God to be our King?

The prophets provided enough information for us to know how Messiah would be born, where he would be born, and now we see why he would be born. Look how intensely Yeshua suffered in order to take the burden of our sin, our self-centeredness and delusions of self-sufficiency—everything that separates us from God. Why did he do it? Because, as he himself said: "Greater love has no one than this, than to lay down one's life for his friends" (John 15:13). That is good news for all of us.

AND YOU?

Is your mind open to seeing your need for Messiah to deal with your sin? Does the love it took for Yeshua to suffer and die for you free you to trust him with your heart? If that makes you uncomfortable, can you admit it? Will you ask God to give you the grace and faith to trust him?

"Behold, the days are coming, declares the LORD, when I will make a new covenant with the house of Israel and the house of Judah, not like the covenant that I made with their fathers on the day when I took them by the hand to bring them out of the land of Egypt, my covenant that they broke, though I was their husband, declares the LORD. For this is the covenant that I will make with the house of Israel after those days, declares the LORD: I will put my law within them, and I will write it on their hearts. And I will be their God, and they shall be my people. And no longer shall each one teach his neighbor and each his brother, saying, 'Know the LORD,' for they shall all know me, from the least of them to the greatest, declares the LORD. For I will forgive their iniquity, and I will remember their sin no more."

Jeremiah 31:31–34 ESV

Messiah would establish a new covenant.

CHAPTER 8

An Ancient Clue
About What's New

Franklin Delano Roosevelt famously accepted his nomination to run for president with the words, "I pledge you, I pledge myself, to a New Deal for the American people." That promise resonated throughout the nation during some of the darkest days in United States history: the Great Depression.

By the time FDR was inaugurated, the nation's banking system had collapsed. Nearly a quarter of the labor force was unemployed, and countless people lost farms and homes due to bankruptcy. Many were hungry and desperate. Roosevelt's New Deal was designed to accomplish three goals for the American people: (economic) relief, recovery, and reform. Although the efficacy of his programs is still debated, his pledge bears a startling resemblance to a promise God made to the Jewish people.

All God's Covenants Are a Big Deal

FDR's pledge was modeled after the ancient concept of covenant. The word *covenant* comes from the Latin *convenire*, which means "to come together." The Hebrew word that translates to "covenant" is *brit* and is often seen in the expression *karat brit*, which means to cut a covenant. Cutting was the basis of ancient near Eastern agreements; animals were literally cut open in a ceremony to illustrate that the covenant was so binding that the life of one who broke it would be forfeit. So, covenants are binding agreements, usually made between individuals, but sometimes between a king and his subjects. In the Bible we see God initiating covenants to create important and enduring relationships.

God made these covenants a matter of permanent and public record. Among them, as we've already mentioned, is the Abrahamic covenant from Genesis 12, which is repeated and passed down to Isaac and Jacob. Later God gave the Mosaic covenant, often called the Torah, or the Sinai covenant (Exodus 19–24), and the Davidic covenant found in 2 Samuel 7.

God's Promise of a New Covenant Changes Everything

Each covenant that God established and implemented in Israel's history was built on previous covenants—but only one covenant was presented in contrast to another: the new covenant. Likewise, the new covenant is the only covenant that God promised to make at a future time. Some other covenants were promising things that had yet to occur. But only the new covenant is mentioned before God actually brings it into being.

This promise of a new covenant was made in some of the darkest days of Israel's monarchy. Ten of the twelve tribes of Israel had been conquered and carried off into captivity by the Assyrians. Judah and especially Jerusalem, her capital, were now facing a similar fate at the hands of the Babylonians. God had appointed the prophet Jeremiah to describe even darker days that lay ahead. But, in the midst of these dire predictions, God gave Jeremiah some glorious news to share. He shone this bright and hopeful promise of a new covenant as a ray of light to pierce the darkness.

Jeremiah 31 is the only place in all the Hebrew Scriptures that mentions the new covenant (in Hebrew, *brit chadashah*), sometimes called the new testament. In fact, the New Testament portion of the Bible is so named, not because it claims to be better than, or a replacement for the Old Testament Scriptures, but rather because it unfolds the fulfillment of this sacred promise found in Jeremiah.

What Jewish Tradition Says About the New Covenant

Interestingly, the Talmud makes no reference to this promise. But we do find allusions to it in Jewish liturgy. For example, a Yom Kippur prayer beginning in Hebrew, *"Titen acharit le'amecha"* includes the request that God make (literally, "cut," echoing biblical phraseology) a new covenant with Israel.[1]

The fact that the hope of a new covenant appears in Jewish liturgy shows that even if Christians used the Jeremiah passage in their own arguments, it still proved a source of a live hope within the Jewish community.[2]

And, while Jewish sources do not assert that the Messiah will actually usher in the new covenant, it has made sense to Jews and Christians alike to associate the Jeremiah passage with the Messiah. Jewish scholar Goshen-Gottstein says, "Both Jews and Christians eventually make this association at some point."[3]

Some rabbinic writings, especially in the context of medieval Christian claims, interpret Jeremiah as speaking of a *renewed* covenant—the same covenant but with a restart. But how is that possible, when the prophecy clearly states that a primary aspect of this new covenant is that it is "*not like* the covenant that I made with their fathers on the day when I took them by the hand to bring them out of the land of Egypt" (Jer. 31:32 ESV, emphasis added)? God is clearly comparing and contrasting this new covenant with the Mosaic covenant. In what ways were the two covenants to be alike and how would the new covenant be different?

The New Covenant Contrasted with the Mosaic Covenant

First, what was the purpose of the Mosaic covenant? To give Israel the opportunity to trust and obey God as his own people, setting them apart as "a kingdom of priests and a holy nation" (Ex. 19:5–6).

Second, where was the Mosaic covenant written? It was written on tablets of stone (Ex. 24:12).

Third, what were the conditions of the Mosaic covenant? If the people would "observe carefully all [God's] commandments," they would receive blessings (enumerated in Deut. 28:1–14). On the other hand, failure to observe the commandments would result in an even longer list of curses (enumerated in Deut. 28:15–68).

Finally, what was the result of the Mosaic covenant?

Despite intermittent times of obedience and blessings, the bottom line is that Israel was not able to keep that covenant; it was broken because of unbelief, because of disobedience. God made that brokenness very clear: "My covenant which they broke, though I was a husband to them, says the LORD" (Jer. 31:32).

If the Mosaic covenant was the only hope for Israel to be blessed, and to be God's special representatives, then hope would have been lost when the covenant was broken. How then would God keep those earlier promises he made to Abraham, Isaac, Jacob, and David? We needed a new covenant!

And we were promised one, in Jeremiah 31.

What then, was the purpose of the new covenant? It was the same purpose as the Mosaic covenant: a relationship. God wanted Israel set apart as his own, a people who would know, love, and follow his ways—a people who would represent the beauty of his holiness to the other nations.

So how was the new covenant different?

Most remarkably, look at where it is written: on the hearts of the people of Israel! That is so important. No longer would God's people express their relationship to him through laborious observance of hundreds of external commandments. Rather, our lives would conform to an inner reality of what it means to know God and to be his people.

What are the conditions of the new covenant? None are mentioned in Jeremiah. However, that doesn't mean there would not be any, so read on! Keep in mind that the covenant had not yet been made, and Jeremiah's description is not giving all the details.

Finally, what is the result of the new covenant? A restored relationship, made possible through forgiveness.

Talk about relief, recovery, and reform! God promised to relieve Israel of the curses of disobedience, to recover the relationship he'd promised so long ago, and to provide the basis for true reform: not an external list of dos and don'ts, but an understanding of what God wants and a desire to please him that comes straight from the heart.

Again, Jeremiah does not specify when this new covenant will come into being, only that "the days are coming." Clearly those days would be after the people returned from exile. But nowhere do we read that the exiles who returned to the land experienced this new level of relationship with God, nor do the Hebrew Scriptures mention this covenant again.

The next mention of the new covenant is from Yeshua, in the New Testament. He made an astounding statement about it during what is commonly called the Last Supper, shortly before he was executed.

Yeshua's Passover Announcement

Yeshua had gathered his closest followers to celebrate Passover, the Festival of Redemption. He had already told them that he would not be with them much longer. He had already explained that the Son of Man (a messianic title that he used in referring to himself) had not come to be served, but to serve and to give his life for others. This must have been extremely discomforting for the disciples on what normally would have been a joyous occasion.

If you have celebrated Passover yourself, you know that it's all about how God redeemed Israel from slavery in Egypt. What you may not have seen is how key elements of the Passover are ultimately fulfilled in the life and mission of Yeshua. And this is exactly where the promise of a new covenant emerges. I believe that covenant was foreshadowed at the original Passover that occurred in Egypt. But it was more than foreshadowed at the Passover Yeshua celebrated with his disciples: it was literally announced!

After the meal, Jesus took a piece of *matzah* (unleavened bread), gave thanks for it, then broke it and passed it to his disciples, saying, "This is my body which is given for you; do this in remembrance of Me" (Luke 22:19). After he had taken the bread, Yeshua picked up "the cup."

At Passover, everyone drinks from their cup four times. Each time, the cup is called by a different name to underscore a specific meaning. A highlight of the Passover celebration is when the piece of matzah is followed by the third cup, which is called "the cup of redemption." Luke 22:20 quotes the announcement Yeshua made at that point. He raised the cup after supper and declared, "This cup is the new covenant in My blood."

In other words, during the Passover celebration, Jesus applied the cup of redemption to himself as he announced that his blood was ratifying the new covenant.

Yeshua's disciples had already realized that their rabbi was the Messiah (Matt. 16:16). Now he's chosen the Festival of Redemption to announce that the days that Jeremiah said "are coming" were finally here.

There's just one problem: how did talk of Jesus' blood and upcoming death fit into the Messiah ushering in the new covenant? We can only imagine what a strange combination of joy and sorrow, anticipation and dread Yeshua's words must have stirred. But it wasn't until he returned from the grave and opened their minds that they were able to see what he meant.

Now that the day of the new covenant had come, it was time to reveal the requirement for making it. Covenants were most often confirmed in blood and that was true of the new covenant as well.

Yeshua was about to lay down his life and allow his blood to be shed as the ultimate condition upon which the new covenant rested. And in his act of self-sacrifice, he put an end to the need for any other blood sacrifice . . . because he did what all the other sacrifices could only point to.

Why the Ultimate Sacrifice Had to Be Yeshua

Yeshua was the only one who had kept the Law perfectly, the one to whom only blessing and no curses was due. And that is why he was able to take upon himself the curses for each and every person who had broken God's law. Just as death passed over the homes marked by the blood of the Passover lamb as described in the book of Exodus, so the blood of Yeshua marks each of us who identify with him, rescuing us from spiritual death. The blood Yeshua shed to bring in the new covenant was a fulfillment of the Passover and every other promise offered through the Torah. That's why he said:

> Truly, truly, I say to you, whoever hears my word and believes him who sent me has eternal life. He does not come into judgment, but has passed from death to life. (John 5:24 ESV)

No longer would daily offerings of animals in the temple be needed to atone for sin. No longer would the Jewish people have to wait in suspense on Yom Kippur to see if the high priest would emerge from the holy of holies as a sign that God had forgiven the sins of the people. Once and for all, atonement would be made for all who will admit their need and trust in God's provision.

When Yeshua died on the cross, the veil that separated everyone but the high priest from the holy of holies in the temple was torn from top to bottom. This indicated that he made it possible for us to have access to the Holy One of Israel. And that includes Gentiles.

Remember, God began revealing the mission of the Messiah back in Genesis 3:15, before the Jewish people existed. As soon as the first human beings distrusted and disobeyed God, he pronounced the curse of sin and predicted the cure for sin. Little by little, the predictions became more and more specific as the portrait of the coming Messiah began taking shape. All the nations of the world were to be blessed through the Jewish people—the people through whom God promised a redeemer. And he delivered his promises in the person of Yeshua.[4]

And yet the disciples, who knew the prophecies and who had spent three years with the Messiah, still needed him to open their minds to understand his mission.

AND YOU?

Like the disciples, our minds can be so focused on what we think ought to happen that we are not always open to see what actually *is* happening. What is God doing? He's offering forgiveness through Yeshua. He's offering a new covenant where he relieves us of all our frustration and failed attempts at being self-sovereigns who ignore God's rightful rule in our lives. He offers restoration by forgiving us because someone else took the consequences of our rebellion. And he offers reform by writing in our hearts all we need to know to live for him, and to live with joy and purpose as his people.

How does that affect you? If you have a gnawing feeling that this new covenant, this New Deal isn't for you because you really don't want God to rule in your heart, then guess what? You are not alone! God understands that we struggle to accept his rightful place in our lives, and he built the solution right into this covenant. God patiently waits for people he created and loves, both Jewish and Gentile, to admit the truth and ask for his help. Are you willing to tell God that you simply can't give him what he deserves unless or until he changes your heart? If you are, you can ask to be part of his new covenant. You can ask him to change you from the inside out, based on Yeshua's death and resurrection.

SECTION 3

Clues About Messiah in the Writings

The third section of the Hebrew Bible is called *Ketuvim* or Writings. These include the "Five Scrolls," the Scriptures that we read on Jewish holidays, along with other books. Here we find books such as Proverbs with its words of wisdom and historical accounts such as Ezra and Nehemiah. But above all, here we have the book of Psalms, which has furnished so much of the synagogue liturgy as well as inspiring hope in the hearts of countless individuals.

The Psalms are prayers to God. They speak of personal affliction and national hopes; they reflect emotions of anger, trust, depression, elation, disappointment, and longing. In the midst of all this outpouring of feeling, certain psalms offer glimpses of a coming redeemer. Psalm 2 speaks of the future Messiah as a king. Psalm 16 intimates that he will overcome even the grave itself. Psalm 22 portrays sufferings from which he would emerge victorious, while Psalm 110 highlights his role as not just a king but also a priest, enabling him to mediate between God and people. As the psalmists articulate their emotions and hopes, the same future person that we find in the Torah and the Prophets reappears, showing that the hope of redemption continues on in the heart of Israel.

Why do the nations rage
and the peoples plot in vain?
The kings of the earth set themselves,
and the rulers take counsel together,
against the LORD *and against his Anointed, saying,*
"Let us burst their bonds apart
and cast away their cords from us."

He who sits in the heavens laughs;
the Lord holds them in derision.
Then he will speak to them in his wrath,
and terrify them in his fury, saying,
"As for me, I have set my King
on Zion, my holy hill."

I will tell of the decree:
The LORD *said to me, "You are my Son;*
today I have begotten you.
Ask of me, and I will make the nations your heritage,
and the ends of the earth your possession.
You shall break them with a rod of iron
and dash them in pieces like a potter's vessel."

Now therefore, O kings, be wise;
be warned, O rulers of the earth.
Serve the LORD *with fear,*
and rejoice with trembling.
Kiss the Son,
lest he be angry, and you perish in the way,
for his wrath is quickly kindled.
Blessed are all who take refuge in him.

Psalm 2 ESV

Messiah would be the Son of God.

CHAPTER 9

King Messiah, God's Own Son

I was handing out our gospel pamphlets in New York City many years ago when a clean-shaven man in a nice suit strode purposefully toward me. His eyes were livid, and his face was tight with rage.

The words that poured out of his mouth were in sharp contrast to his neat and professional appearance. I won't repeat the crude accusations, but he was pouring contempt on the idea of God having offspring, much less a baby who needed to have his diapers changed, etc.

Recently, I was recounting the incident with my colleague Ruth Rosen, and was amazed by her response. Years ago, she received a series of voicemail messages from an enraged caller who used the identical explicit language. We agreed that her anonymous caller was probably the same guy who had vented his rage at me that day on the street corner.

That wasn't the end of the story, but for now, let's look at what had this guy so riled up: the idea that you can be Jewish and believe that God has a son.

Does God Really Have a Son?

This is a thorny issue for most Jewish people who believe in God, and it tends to inspire two types of responses. Some say, "Of course God has a son because we're all God's children." Others point out how the Bible sometimes refers to Israel as God's son. Or how, on occasion, God referred to some of the kings of Bible times as his sons.

But it's a different matter if we are speaking about *the* Son of God as a unique individual who acts on God's behalf as no one else can—because he embodies the divine nature and character of God. In that case, the traditional Jewish response is "Absolutely not!" After all, we affirm with all our hearts, "Hear, O Israel: The LORD our God, the LORD is one!" (Deut. 6:4).

This concept of God having *a* Son (meaning one and only one specific person) was shocking for the Jewish people, even in Bible times. And yet, throughout the Hebrew Scriptures the Messiah is described as so much more than merely human. And in some places, especially Psalm 2, we see a claim of a unique individual who is God's eternal Son, sharing his nature, offering salvation, and representing the Father as the hero in the greatest cosmic conflict in history. Neither Israel as a nation nor any one king of Israel comes close to fulfilling such an amazing role.

Yeshua Claimed to Be God's Son

These controversial assertions were (and still are) central to Yeshua's claims. For example, in the gospel of John we read how Yeshua not only continually referred to God as his Father, but actually said, "I and My Father are one" (John 10:30). I imagine when he appeared to his earliest followers after his resurrection so unexpectedly and opened their minds, he clarified how Hebrew Scriptures pointed to that unique relationship.

And today, if we consider Yeshua's controversial claim with an open mind, the biblical evidence is compelling.

In the book of Proverbs, the idea of God's Son is posed as a riddle:

> Who but God goes up to heaven and comes back down?
> Who holds the wind in his fists?
> Who wraps up the oceans in his cloak?
> Who has created the whole wide world?
> What is his name—and his son's name?
> Tell me if you know! (Prov. 30:4 NLT)

King David's Perspective

In Psalm 2 the author, King David, speaks pointedly and prophetically about this unique son.

When reading the psalm, it's helpful to know that Psalm 1 and 2 were probably composed as a unity, and later divided into two separate songs or poems. Both paint a stark contrast between the righteous and the wicked.

Psalm 1 uses the word *ashrei* (blessed) to describe the man who is righteous. Psalm 2 ends with the promise of the same blessing to those who trust in the righteous man, who is none other than Messiah.

Psalm 1 introduces us to the righteous one who meditates on and delights in God's Torah, in contrast to the wicked who do not. Psalm 2 begins with a question about those same wicked ones, "Why do the nations rage and the peoples plot in vain?" (ESV). The wicked people and their rulers "band together against the LORD and against his anointed" (Ps. 2:2 NIV) Here the Hebrew word for "anointed" is *mashiach*, from which we get the word *Messiah*.

One medieval rabbinic midrash (exposition) on this verse made the following comment on those whom the psalmist described as being "Against God and his Messiah."

> "Against God and his Messiah," likening them to a robber
> who stands defiantly behind the palace of the King and
> says, "If I shall find the son of the King, I shall lay hold of
> him, and kill him, and crucify him, and make him die a cruel
> death." But the Holy Spirit mocks him, "He that sits in the
> heavens laughs."[1]

God's first response to the rebellion of those wicked people is laughter, scoffing, and rebuke of their arrogance and evil intentions—after all, it *is* laughable to imagine that a human plot against God could succeed. But then God takes action. From his throne in heaven, God introduces his anointed one. And we see that his earthly King is also the "Blessed One" of Psalm 1.

Having been introduced by God in heaven, Messiah now speaks, saying,

> I will tell of the decree:
> The LORD said to me, "You are my Son;
> today I have begotten you." (Ps. 2:7 ESV)

Talk about shocking—this is one of the most startling passages in the entire Hebrew Scriptures! This is the Messiah, the Anointed One talking about the LORD's decree. And note, whenever you see "LORD" capitalized this way, it refers to the sacred covenant name of God. (In some Bibles, it is translated as Jehovah or Yahweh.) The Messiah is saying that God himself has decreed that he (Messiah) is God's own begotten Son.

This prophecy turns the whole concept of the Messiah's nature on its head. While other prophecies raise questions about the eternal nature and divine power of the Messiah, this one provides a meaningful resolution.

We Can't Have the Father Without the Son

The psalmist tells us that anyone honoring the Son is in alignment with the Father. They are one and the same—which is exactly what Jesus claimed.

There has only ever been one man who is truly righteous. The rest of us may try, but as we saw in Isaiah 53, we all fall short. The Messiah, on the other hand, is the true Son of God as well as the righteous man. That is why he stands with the Father in heaven both to judge the people and call them to repentance and faith. That is why he has the power to pronounce forgiveness. That is why those who choose to "serve the LORD with fear" (Ps. 2:11) will ultimately choose to kiss (pay homage to) the Son.

You will see echoes of this psalm no less than six times throughout the New Testament. Perhaps the most poignant and pointed example was when John was baptizing Yeshua in the Jordan River. As the Son of God went down into the water and came back up, the Scripture describes a voice from heaven announcing, "You are my beloved Son; in You I am well pleased" (Luke 3:22). And the Spirit of God descended upon him in the form of a dove. That is one of the clearest evidences of the complex unity of God, also referred to the triune nature of God, or the Trinity.

The Unity of God Is Absolute . . . and Complex

There is only one God, but God is a unity within himself. The Hebrew Scriptures speak of God, the Spirit of God, and now the Son of God.

This is hinted at yet hidden in the Hebrew Scriptures, and ultimately revealed in the New Testament. The early Jewish believers in Jesus had seen fragments of this truth in their own Scriptures, but now they were seeing it before them in the person of Jesus. "These are the words which I spoke to you while I was still with you, that all things must be fulfilled which were written in the Law of Moses and the Prophets and the Psalms concerning Me" (Luke 24:44). This was part of the message of the early church that Paul and Peter were preaching.

The author of Hebrews, which was written to early Jewish believers in Jesus, also refers to Psalm 2: "For to which of the angels did God ever say, 'You are my Son, today I have begotten you'? Or again, 'I will be to him a father, and he shall be to me a son'?" (Heb. 1:5 ESV).

Standing with the Son Gives Comfort and Courage

The prediction that Messiah would be the Son of God was essential to Yeshua's first-century followers' understanding of his identity back then, just as it is to his followers today. The psalm provided the knowledge, strength, and comfort those early followers of Jesus needed when they experienced opposition and even persecution for their faith.

For example, Peter and John were two of the earliest disciples whose minds Yeshua had opened. As a result, they had opened thousands of other people's minds to the risen Messiah, even performing miracles in his name. This upset the Sadducees, a sect of religious authorities, who took them into overnight custody to be questioned the next day. When they could find no fault with Yeshua's followers, they released them with a severe command not to speak any more about Yeshua.

But Peter and John refused to comply, because they were compelled to speak by a greater authority. They gave honor to God,

> who through the mouth of our father David, your servant, said by the Holy Spirit, "Why did the Gentiles rage, and the peoples plot in vain? The kings of the earth set themselves, and the rulers were gathered together, against the Lord and against his Anointed"—for truly in this city there were gathered together against your holy servant Jesus, whom you anointed, both Herod and Pontius Pilate, along with the Gentiles and the peoples of Israel, to do whatever your hand and your plan had predestined to take place. (Acts 4:25–28 ESV)

The disciples who were once filled with doubts and questions were now unstoppable, urging people to repent and receive the forgiveness made possible by Yeshua. They recognized the cosmic conflict depicted in Psalm 2. That conflict has continued across the globe and in every generation to this day.

Like those early disciples, when we align ourselves with Yeshua, we are doing so by order of God the Father. He wants us to show where we stand with him by taking a stand with his Messiah. Doing so may incur the anger of others who, like in Psalm 2, are rebelling against God, and by extension, against his Son, the Messiah. It may even incur the anger of people who believe they are loyal to God, but have not yet embraced what his Word says about the Messiah.

Either way, if you have the courage to identify with the Son of God, you can expect some level of opposition. You might never be detained or jailed for your faith, but some will regard you as foolish or worse. How many times have I heard, "Don't be ridiculous, God doesn't have a son." Well, it was predicted in the Jewish Bible. This is exactly who the Messiah is.

According to the psalmist, God expects us to embrace that truth, to "kiss" the Son, to pay homage, to love and adore him as the Messiah of God. And when you do so, you can count on sharing in the joy and comfort found here in the very same psalm, "Blessed are all who take refuge in him" (Ps. 2:12 ESV). That promise of blessing outweighs any opposition you might face.

An Unexpected Change of Heart

I'd like to conclude the story I started at the beginning of this chapter, about the man on the street who was so enraged. Years after that rant, as well as the series of angry voicemail messages he'd left my colleague, he called and left her a very different message.

He began by identifying himself as the person who had left hateful and vile messages. He went on to apologize for his words, not only via voicemail, but for the encounters he'd had with Jews for Jesus (like me) in person. Perhaps you can guess what brought about his change of heart.

This man had stopped his raging when he finally came to believe for himself that Yeshua is the Messiah and the son of God. He had "kissed the Son." Now instead of anger, he was filled with understanding, repentance, and peace.

AND YOU?

Maybe you have had a similar change of heart in your faith journey. If so, what did it take to change your anger to openness? Maybe you are still uncertain about who Yeshua is. If you are struggling over whether he is the Messiah, is it because you don't want to risk want to offending God if it's not true? Or is it because you don't want to risk offending other people? If you are most concerned with offending God, are you willing to ask him to help you know the truth about Yeshua, and for the courage to believe it when he does?

YOU WILL NOT ABANDON MY SOUL

A Michtam of David.

Preserve me, O God, for in You I put my trust.

O my soul, you have said to the LORD,
"You are my Lord,
My goodness is nothing apart from You."
As for the saints who are on the earth,
"They are the excellent ones, in whom is all my delight."

Their sorrows shall be multiplied who hasten after another god;
Their drink offerings of blood I will not offer,
Nor take up their names on my lips.

O LORD, You are the portion of my inheritance and my cup;
You maintain my lot.
The lines have fallen to me in pleasant places;
Yes, I have a good inheritance.

I will bless the LORD who has given me counsel;
My heart also instructs me in the night seasons.
I have set the LORD always before me;
Because He is at my right hand I shall not be moved.

Therefore my heart is glad, and my glory rejoices;
My flesh also will rest in hope.
For You will not leave my soul in Sheol,
Nor will You allow Your Holy One to see corruption.
You will show me the path of life;
In Your presence is fullness of joy;
At Your right hand are pleasures forevermore.

Psalm 16

Messiah would be resurrected.

CHAPTER 10

Hope Beyond the Grave

I was on a flight from Paris to San Francisco when the man seated behind me began gasping for air. The flight attendant administered oxygen, but to no avail. An announcement calling for a medical professional came over the intercom, and soon a doctor and several nurses had gathered to help this man.

The pilot announced that due to a medical emergency the plane was going to land in Edmonton—but we never did. The efforts of the doctor and nurses became frantic as they took turns doing CPR. I heard the sound of air being forced out of this man's lungs, and then came the horrific sounds of the death rattle. Finally, the doctor pronounced time of death.

The captain came back on the intercom and announced that the passenger's "situation had stabilized" and that we were continuing to San Francisco. Only a few passengers saw the flight attendants pull a blanket over the dead man's head, but many could hear his dear wife, still seated next to him, crying in anguish, sometimes sobbing, sometimes moaning as the flight continued.

Suddenly the flight attendants were coming down the aisles serving lunch. Lunch? How could any of us eat after what had just happened? In all fairness to the flight attendants, they handled a dreadful situation very professionally and did their best to help people regain a degree of normalcy.

I've often thought of that airplane cabin as a metaphor for the world we live in. As we journey together through life, people die every day. Some of us have not yet experienced the sights and sounds and smells of death, while others have recollections of such things emblazoned in our memories. Many of us are broken over the pain and loss of a loved one's death. Others struggle with the reality of our own impending demise. Then there are those who are just trying to go on with "normal" life, pretending not to see, trying to avoid noticing the grim realities surrounding them.

Biblical Hope in the Face of Death

Staring death in the face is one of the most unsettling and difficult passages of life. The Bible addresses the reality of death head on and doesn't sugarcoat it. But it does give us an antidote to the worst of our fears.

Do you fear death? Most people do, even if they put up a brave front when discussing the topic. In this prophecy in Psalm 16, King David models a remarkable disposition toward death. In so doing, he foreshadows the great hope he had in the promise of Messiah, who would conquer the power of death for all humanity.

The Context of Psalm 16

Psalm 16 is inscribed as a "Miktam of David." We don't know what the word *Miktam* means—perhaps it was an ancient musical notation. We *do* know that the other Miktams of David (Psalms 56–60) are "fugitive" psalms; David wrote them while on the run from or facing attack from his enemies. It has been suggested that David wrote this particular psalm while he was fleeing from Saul (1 Sam. 21:10).

Have you ever felt like the whole world is against you—as though seemingly insurmountable adversities have beaten you down, leaving you vulnerable and alone? David was facing that kind of physical and emotional stress when he wrote this psalm. In light of this, his confident tone is quite stunning: "Preserve me, O God, for in You I put my trust" (v. 1).

In the midst of relentless life-threatening pursuit, David's confidence was secure because it was built on his trust in God. His life embodied a relationship of commitment and obedience to the one who alone had the power to preserve his life. Forced to flee, having lost his home, his loved ones, and all outward signs of security, David laid claim to the only sure possession he had left: "O LORD, You are the portion of my inheritance and my cup" (v. 5).

Focusing on God Guarantees We'll Stay on Course

Centuries earlier, God told Aaron and the other priests, "You shall have no inheritance in their land, nor shall you have any portion among them; I am your portion and your inheritance among the children of Israel" (Num. 18:20). So too, David knew that he didn't need land or possessions to have a lasting inheritance. He desired God more than anything, and was confident that God was his "portion."

It may be natural to feel forgotten or abandoned in life's harshest situations and circumstances. We might find it hard to know which way to turn or whom we can trust. But amazingly,

David wrote with great certainty about his direction and his destiny: "I have set the LORD always before me; because He is at my right hand I shall not be moved" (v. 8).

David knew something then that is still true today. The one way to be sure of our direction in life is to keep the Lord directly before us—meaning to focus on following him. Do that and you can rest assured he is at your side, by your right hand as well. God is better than any GPS on the road of life.

But notice that David's confidence extended beyond this temporal plane with all its trouble and woe—he had hope that passes beyond this life into the next.

How do we journey from this life into the next with the same confidence David expressed? How can we know that one day we will arrive at God's right hand as well, and experience his presence in an amazing array of pleasures forevermore (v. 11)?

The answer is found in David's hope of the resurrection: "For You will not leave my soul in Sheol, nor will You allow Your Holy One to see corruption" (v. 10).[1]

Who Is God's Holy One?

"Holy One" (*hasid* in Hebrew) comes from the Hebrew root *hesed*, a multifaceted word that conveys faithful or covenant love, which includes loyalty, kindness, mercy, and grace. A Hasid (translated *pious* in English) would be one who experiences God's *hesed*. This psalm announces that the Lord's *hasidekha*, his *hasid*, his holy one, would not remain in the grave, subject to a state of corruption.

Everyone dies. We all know that. David knew that he would face death one day. Sooner or later he was destined for Sheol (here referring not to hell but rather to the grave). But he also knew that

God would not *leave* him there. Death, the grave, corruption—this is not the final destination of those who put their hope in God.

How did David command such amazing confidence in a life beyond the grave? He saw in his own life a foreshadowing of the messianic hope. He had been anointed the king of Israel, but another, greater anointed one was to come from David's line.

The key to understanding Psalm 16 is the answer to the question: Who is the "Hasid" or the "Holy One" David refers to in this Scripture?

David knew himself to be *a* hasid. He refers to his piety, his holiness in numerous places, including 2 Samuel 22:21–25 and Psalm 4:3. But the prophets used terms like the Lord's "servant" and his "anointed one" both to refer to their contemporaries and to speak prophetically of the one who will more fully embody those terms. The Scripture uses the term *Hasid* in the same way. This psalm anticipates the fulfillment of the person, office, and mission of the holy One who was yet to come—the Hasid it foreshadowed was the Messiah.[2]

Of course, Psalm 16 is not solely messianic; it expresses King David's hope that God would rescue *him* from death—and God did, on numerous occasions. But ultimately, David did die, and his body did go into the grave, where it remained. Today you can visit the place believed by many to be his tomb. It's in the city of Jerusalem, just across the Kidron Valley.

The Famous Sermon from This Psalm

According to ancient Jewish tradition, David not only was born but also died on the festival of Pentecost (*Shavuot* in Hebrew). That is why religious Jews still gather by the thousands to pray at the tomb of David during Shavuot.

With that tradition in mind, Peter, one of Yeshua's most ardent followers, confidently stood and testified in Jerusalem on Shavuot. He drew the crowd's attention to Psalm 16 as he spoke about King David, the resurrection, and Jesus:

> "Men and brethren, let me speak freely to you of the patriarch David, that he is both dead and buried, and his tomb is with us to this day. Therefore, being a prophet, and knowing that God had sworn an oath to him that of the fruit of his body, according to the flesh, He would raise up the [Messiah] to sit on his throne, he, foreseeing this, spoke concerning the resurrection of the [Messiah], that His soul was not left in [Sheol], nor did His flesh see corruption. This Jesus God has raised up." (Acts 2:29–32)

In other words, if David is dead and buried in a nearby grave, then what about his declaration that God would not allow his holy one to be abandoned to the grave or to experience the corruption that comes after death? Although David himself would not be forever abandoned to the grave (meaning he would one day experience resurrection), by that point his body had certainly seen the corruption that comes after death.

Clearly the second part of that declaration must be fully realized in another Hasid. David, a holy one of God, had unfettered confidence in his future resurrection—because it was rooted and grounded in the promise of the resurrection of a greater holy one, the Hasid, Messiah Yeshua, also known as the Son of David.

As Peter, a fisherman from Galilee, drove home this point from the Scriptures, about three thousand Jewish people who heard the message became followers of Messiah Yeshua.

What had changed Peter so radically? On the night that Jesus was arrested Peter was so terrified of meeting the same fate that he denied even knowing his master. Now he (along with the other disciples) was boldly, publicly proclaiming Jesus as Messiah to whoever would listen.

No doubt seeing Yeshua alive once more gave his followers joy and confidence to spread the good news. But the crowds needed more than that. In order to follow Yeshua, they needed to know that he was the one of whom the Scriptures spoke. That is why Yeshua had opened his disciples' minds to understand the Scriptures before sending them out to deliver the good news that he had conquered death. Just like Jesus had told them before he was crucified, his death would be turned upside down, and used to achieve life—like the grain of wheat falls into the earth and dies in order to multiply and bear fruit (John 12:24).

As the pieces of various messianic prophecies came together, Yeshua's resurrection could be seen in context, and it took on a most powerful and personal meaning.

Jesus Contrasted with Others Who Came Back from Death

After all, if the Bible is true, Jesus was not the first person to come back from the dead. In the Hebrew Scriptures, we read accounts of two prophets, Elijah and Elisha, each bringing a child who had died back to life. Jesus himself is said to have raised people from the dead as well. But eventually, each of those who came back to life would end up back in the grave once more. So, while it's impressive that Yeshua rose from the dead, why would it give his followers so much boldness and hope?

Yeshua alone came back from the grave *never to die again!* His resurrection, unlike the others, was proof that death had no power over him. Remember Genesis 3: death entered the world because of sin. Sin separates us from God, and that separation is really what death is all about. It wasn't enough to know where Messiah would be born, or what his lineage would be, or even that he would have a miraculous birth. People needed to know, as mentioned in chapter 7, that the Messiah who had no sin would die for the sins of others. And this is where it becomes personal.

We are invited to identify with Yeshua's death by acknowledging that our own sin separates us from God, and that Messiah died to take our place. The good news is, when we turn from our sin and identify with Messiah in his death, we receive his life, including the promise of resurrection!

That is why Yeshua's resurrection is described as "the first fruits" of those who have died but will one day be brought back to life (1 Cor. 15), alluding to the first fruits offerings that were part of the biblical harvest festivals. Those offerings were just the beginning of the greater harvest to come.

Freedom from Fear

King David wrote another psalm that has comforted countless people in the face of death. You probably know or at least have heard it: Psalm 23. Like David, even when life takes you through the valley of the shadow of death, you need fear no evil. The confident hope of dwelling in the house of the Lord forever is linked to the belief that the grave will not be the end of our story. That confidence, that hope, is available to you, to me, and to anyone who will believe and trust in Yeshua's death and resurrection on their behalf.

AND YOU?

If you believe in Yeshua, how has his resurrection changed your approach to life? If you are unsure whether Yeshua is the Messiah, are you willing to ask God to open your mind to the possibility that Yeshua conquered death so that you can look forward to eternal life with him?

My God, My God, why have You forsaken Me?
Why are You so far from helping Me,
And from the words of My groaning?
O My God, I cry in the daytime, but You do not hear;
And in the night season, and am not silent.

But You are holy,
Enthroned in the praises of Israel.
Our fathers trusted in You;
They trusted, and You delivered them.
They cried to You, and were delivered;
They trusted in You, and were not ashamed.

But I am a worm, and no man;
A reproach of men, and despised by the people.
All those who see Me ridicule Me;
They shoot out the lip, they shake the head, saying,
"He trusted in the LORD, let Him rescue Him;
Let Him deliver Him, since He delights in Him!"

But You are He who took Me out of the womb;
You made Me trust while on My mother's breasts.
I was cast upon You from birth.
From My mother's womb
You have been My God.
Be not far from Me,
For trouble is near;
For there is none to help.

Many bulls have surrounded Me;
Strong bulls of Bashan have encircled Me.
They gape at Me with their mouths,
Like a raging and roaring lion.

I am poured out like water,
And all My bones are out of joint;
My heart is like wax;
It has melted within Me.
My strength is dried up like a potsherd,
And My tongue clings to My jaws;
You have brought Me to the dust of death.

For dogs have surrounded Me;
The congregation of the wicked has enclosed Me.
They pierced My hands and My feet;
I can count all My bones.
They look and stare at Me.
They divide My garments among them,
And for My clothing they cast lots.

But You, O Lord, *do not be far from Me;*
O My Strength, hasten to help Me!
Deliver Me from the sword,
My precious life from the power of the dog.
Save Me from the lion's mouth
And from the horns of the wild oxen!

You have answered Me.

I will declare Your name to My brethren;
In the midst of the assembly I will praise You.
You who fear the Lord, *praise Him!*
All you descendants of Jacob, glorify Him,
And fear Him, all you offspring of Israel!
For He has not despised nor abhorred the affliction of the afflicted;
Nor has He hidden His face from Him;
But when He cried to Him, He heard.
My praise shall be of You in the great assembly;

I will pay My vows before those who fear Him.
The poor shall eat and be satisfied;
Those who seek Him will praise the LORD.
Let your heart live forever!

All the ends of the world
Shall remember and turn to the LORD,
And all the families of the nations
Shall worship before You.
For the kingdom is the LORD's,
And He rules over the nations.

All the prosperous of the earth
Shall eat and worship;
All those who go down to the dust
Shall bow before Him,
Even he who cannot keep himself alive.

A posterity shall serve Him.
It will be recounted of the Lord to the next generation,
They will come and declare His righteousness to a people who will be born,
That He has done this.

Psalm 22

Messiah would be forsaken and tortured, but snatched from the jaws of defeat.

CHAPTER 11

Famous Last Words

When I lived in Chicago, I met a Jewish attorney who was interested in studying the life of Jesus. I suggested he read through Matthew's account, and for several months we met weekly, drinking coffee and discussing what he'd read. One day he seemed particularly eager to get to the point without any of our usual small talk. As soon as we sat down, he blurted out, "David, now I know that Jesus cannot be the Messiah."

"Really?" I responded. "Why is that?"

"Because this week I read what he said when he was hanging on the cross. He said, 'My God, My God, why have You forsaken Me?' (Matt. 27:46). Now what kind of a Messiah would say something like that to God?"

"Ah," I responded. "I agree that sounds like an angry, maybe even desperate accusation. But before you decide, let's look at the back story." Then I turned to the very prophecy we are looking at now, Psalm 22. There we see that Jesus' agonized question as he hung on the cross was not a bitter slip of the tongue, but a very intentional quote from the first verse of this psalm.

I pointed out to my friend that while the majority of the Psalms were written by King David some one thousand years before the birth of Yeshua, most of those psalms were very familiar to Jewish people. Many, including this one, had been set to the tune of an already popular song.

So when Yeshua called out the first verse of Psalm 22 (v. 2 in the Hebrew Bible), it was almost like singing the first few bars of a hit song from the billboard charts. He intended it to point to the entire song. In the midst of his agony, Yeshua demonstrated the predictive nature of what David had written so long before—and its amazing correspondence to all he was suffering in that moment.

In fact, it was not just the words Yeshua quoted—*"Eli, Eli, lama sabachtani?"*[1] (My God, my God, why have you forsaken me?), but the entire psalm that very specifically prophesied the crucifixion Yeshua was enduring.

As I sat with my attorney friend that day reading through Psalm 22, he was visibly shocked. He had assumed that Yeshua's words proved that he could not be the Messiah. Instead, those words confronted him with compelling evidence to the contrary.

It was my turn to be shocked when he responded, "You know what I think? I think Jesus' followers must have put those words in his mouth on purpose to support their own narrative. I don't believe he said those words at all."

"Wait," I said. "A few minutes ago, you were certain that those words were proof positive that Jesus couldn't be the Messiah. Now you are telling me you don't believe he actually said them at all? What changed? How did you arrive at that conclusion?"

We went back and forth but never came to agreement. That meeting concluded his "discovery process" at least for the time; when I called to set up our next meeting, he thanked me and said he had studied enough about Jesus. He was not interested in further discussion. I have thought a lot about that, and what it might mean about belief, unbelief, and the risks and rewards of an open mind. And it has made me eager to walk with you through the rest of Psalm 22 and how it affects our understanding of the Messiah.

Why Yeshua Suffered

Think back to that room full of followers when Jesus "opened their minds to understand the Scriptures" (Luke 24:45 ESV). All of them had either seen firsthand or heard the firsthand account of Jesus' cruel death on that Roman cross. It had stunned and no doubt devastated them. Several were recorded as sadly confessing, "But we were hoping that it was He who was going to redeem Israel" (Luke 24:21). Yeshua's death had dashed that hope to pieces, or so it seemed. They must have wondered why things had taken such a terrible turn.

But now he was standing in front of them, opening their minds to realize that his torturous death was not the end of all hope for redemption. In fact, it was because of that death that all the hope and all the promises concerning Messiah actually could be fulfilled.

Yeshua lived a life that was wholly innocent; he was totally undeserving of the cruel sentence that had been reserved for criminals. That is why his execution and his alone could fulfill the promise of the prophets and the plan of God for our forgiveness and redemption. Through being forsaken by God as he hung on that cross, Yeshua accomplished the most amazing rescue of humanity imaginable.

Talk about a paradox! There is something so beautiful about the life and teachings of Jesus, and yet he willingly submitted himself to such an ugly, undeserved death—the very death of the innocent in place of the guilty that Isaiah predicted. When Yeshua uttered those opening words from Psalm 22, he showed just how great his love for us was. All of us have sinned and separated ourselves from God, and are destined to be left to ourselves, forsaken by him. Jesus chose to endure that separation. He chose to be forsaken by his own Father on our behalf. And you can see the details of how that played out as they were predicted by the author of this psalm: King David.

David himself had endured all kinds of difficult situations, and certainly this psalm was an authentic cry of his heart in the midst of extreme hardship. Yet he had never experienced the full extent of the agony that he wrote about in this psalm. The text provides an amazing confluence of specific events that would later be revealed as a divine prediction of what Yeshua would suffer.

Compare Psalm 22 to Yeshua's Suffering

Look at what the Gospels say about Jesus' experience and see the incredible parallels with Psalm 22.

For example:

> And those who passed by derided him, wagging their heads and saying, "You who would destroy the temple and rebuild it in three days, save yourself! If you are the Son of God, come down from the cross." So also the chief priests, with the scribes and elders, mocked him, saying, "He saved others; he cannot save himself. He is the King of Israel; let him come down now from the cross, and we will believe in him. He trusts in God; let God deliver him now, if he desires him. For he said, 'I am the Son of God.'" (Matt. 27:39–43 ESV)

This is almost an exact enactment of David's words in Psalm 22:7–8: "All who see me mock me; they make mouths at me; they wag their heads; 'He trusts in the LORD; let him deliver him; let him rescue him, for he delights in him!'" (ESV).

Another parallel is found in the gospel of John:

> Then the soldiers, when they had crucified Jesus, took His garments and made four parts, to each soldier a part, and also the tunic. Now the tunic was without seam, woven from the top in one piece. They said therefore among themselves, "Let us not tear it, but cast lots for it, whose it shall be," that the Scripture might be fulfilled which says:
>
> "They divided My garments among them,
> And for My clothing they cast lots."
>
> Therefore the soldiers did these things. (John 19:23–24)

Does this mean the soldiers did this on purpose to fulfill prophecy? Of course not. To them, Jesus was a joke and they knew nothing about the Jewish Bible. They were doing what Roman soldiers did—and yet they were also doing exactly what the psalmist had predicted. What are the chances?

But for me, verses 14–17 offer the most remarkable evidence that this psalm predicted Yeshua's crucifixion:

> I am poured out like water,
> and all my bones are out of joint;
> my heart is like wax;
> it is melted within my breast;
> my strength is dried up like a potsherd,
> and my tongue sticks to my jaws;
> you lay me in the dust of death.
>
> For dogs encompass me;
> a company of evildoers encircles me;

they have pierced my hands and feet—
I can count all my bones—
they stare and gloat over me. (Ps. 22:14–17 ESV)

What's so startling about these words is that *King David recorded them before crucifixion had ever been invented as a form of execution.* And yet, doesn't it sound like a remarkable prediction of what was happening to Jesus on the cross? Especially the descriptive phrases, "my bones are out of joint," and "they have pierced my hands and feet—I can count all my bones."

The Controversy of the Pierced Hands and Feet

Some have debated the translation of verses 16–17. In the Jewish Publication Society translation of Psalm 22, instead of "They pierced my hands and my feet," it says "like a lion they are at my hands and feet." The difference between "they pierced" and "like a lion" comes down to whether the original Hebrew text used the letter "yod" or "vav." They look very similar to each other. That one Hebrew letter changes the word *kaaru*, "they pierced," to *kaari*, meaning "like a lion."

If the Hebrew word "they pierced" actually was meant to be translated "like a lion," some might say the parallel with Yeshua's crucifixion is not quite as remarkable. Could it be that the Jewish Publication Society translators preferred the alternative rendering "like a lion they are at my hands and feet" for that very reason?

As with the translation of the Hebrew word *almah* in the Isaiah 7:14 prophecy, the Septuagint, the Greek translation of the Scriptures, sheds some insight. The Hebrew translators of the Septuagint rendered the word as "they pierced" in the Greek. That gives us an official Jewish understanding of the word at that time. "Like a lion they are at my hands and feet" is certainly an alternative rendering, but it was clearly not the viewpoint among the Jewish scholars entrusted with that early translation of Hebrew to Greek.

Frankly, the case for Yeshua being the Messiah does not hang on any one word, because there are so many other points of connection to him. An Israeli named Asaf demonstrated that to me.

A Totally Different Response to the Same Psalm

Around the same time as I was meeting with the attorney, Asaf and I were also meeting weekly, going through messianic prophecies from the Jewish Bible. Asaf prepared by reading each week's passage in Hebrew, and I struggled with my limited Hebrew to prepare as well.

Asaf, in typical Israeli fashion, grew more and more animated as we read through Psalm 22. He repeatedly exclaimed, "Wow! Wow! Wow!" through the entire passage.

When we got to the end, I began to make the case for the Hebrew text being "they pierced" rather than "like a lion." I had carefully restudied the controversy in preparation for our meeting. But Asaf said, "David, it doesn't matter. This psalm is all about Yeshua!" Not many years later he, too, became a follower of Yeshua.

Asaf and so many like him found the predictions revealed in messianic prophecies just as powerful now as they were millennia ago when Jesus himself opened people's minds to understand them.

Delivered from More than the Grave

If your mind is open to what this psalm is saying, you'll be glad to see it goes beyond the graphic prediction of Messiah's gruesome execution. The last ten verses of the song promise joy that triumphs over torture. David insists that though they laid him in the dust of death, he would declare God's goodness to multitudes of others (i.e., in the midst of the congregation). While he was speaking of his own hope of a coming resurrection, King David was also predicting the Messiah. Many people would hear about this tortured one who was snatched from the jaws of defeat. Even those who had not yet been born would one day see God's deliverance through this event.

The amazing thing is, this is not only God's deliverance of the one who cries out at the very beginning, "My God, my God, why have you forsaken me?" This is God's deliverance for you and me as well.

Yeshua endured the worst kind of suffering—not just the physical pain of hanging on the cross, but even worse, he endured the psychological and spiritual pain of being separated from the Father. And he endured it for one reason: so that we would not have to be forsaken.

What was Jesus experiencing when he cried out, "My God, my God, why have You forsaken Me?"? The Father had allowed the crushing consequences of the sins of the whole world to come down on him. Yeshua willingly suffered under that devastating weight. He loved us so much that he died to overcome the very root of our separation from the Father. What an everlasting and powerful demonstration of God's incredible self-sacrificing love!

If we are willing to identify with Messiah in his suffering, we can also share in his victory. In other words, when we understand that Yeshua died because of our sin, when our hearts melt in grateful surrender to his love and mercy, he promises us a new heart (remember Jeremiah 31?), and he gives us hope beyond the grave: "For God so loved the world that He gave His only begotten Son, that whoever believes in Him should not perish, but have everlasting life" (John 3:16).

AND YOU?

No matter what you have been through, no matter what you may be enduring right now or facing in the future, you can find hope and peace and purpose through faith and trust in Yeshua. He paid a high price to make that possible. If you know that you are loved by God and that he will never abandon you, it makes all the difference in the world. If you have yet to experience that difference, again, I hope you will ask God to open your mind to what he wants you to see.

The LORD said to my Lord,
"Sit at My right hand,
Till I make Your enemies Your footstool."
The LORD shall send the rod of Your strength out of Zion.
Rule in the midst of Your enemies!

Your people shall be volunteers
In the day of Your power;
In the beauties of holiness, from the womb of the morning,
You have the dew of Your youth.
The LORD has sworn
And will not relent,
"You are a priest forever
According to the order of Melchizedek."

The Lord is at Your right hand;
He shall execute kings in the day of His wrath.
He shall judge among the nations,
He shall fill the places with dead bodies,
He shall execute the heads of many countries.
He shall drink of the brook by the wayside;
Therefore He shall lift up the head.

Psalm 110

Messiah would be the greatest Prophet, Priest, and King of all time.

CHAPTER 12

Messiah the GOAT

Sports fans enjoy bragging about their favorite athletes, claiming they are the greatest of all time (the GOAT). Some of the athletes enjoy bragging too—like Mohammed Ali, whose claim "I am the greatest" was his signature line. Everyone knew that as great a boxer as Ali was, his bragging was all part of the schtick, part of the show. Because of course, it's just a matter of time before others come along to lay claim to that title.

We like to see our heroes win titles and awards—not just in sports, but in the arts, sciences, and in the sorts of service to humanity that deserve the honor of a Nobel Peace Prize. It's a joy to admire those whose talents and accomplishments are extraordinary, inspirational, and maybe even for a time unrivaled.

But the Bible speaks of one who truly is forever the greatest of all time. No one else will be coming along to surpass him. The Messiah is the only champion who is truly unrivaled, and Psalm 110 gives us a clue about his unparalleled greatness. I find this one of the most intriguing messianic references in all of the Hebrew Scriptures.

The Messiah Is Unrivaled Because . . .

For one thing, this text reveals that Messiah would be a priest. Everyone knew that the Messiah would be a prophet (like Moses) and a king (from David's line), but here we see that Messiah would surpass these two luminaries of Israel's spiritual legacy with this unprecedented triple claim. And if it weren't enough that Messiah would fill all three roles, he would be the greatest of all prophets, priests, and kings.

First, look at this enigmatic phrase: "*the* LORD said to my Lord." King David is telling us of a conversation that the LORD, that is God himself, has with someone else whom David is calling "my Lord."

One Jewish commentary on Psalm 110 relates the following story.

> Rabbi Yudan said in the name of Rabbi Hama, "In the future, the Holy One, blessed be He, will seat the Messiah King at His right hand, as it says, 'The Lord said to my Lord: "Sit at My right hand"' (Psalm 110:1). And Abraham will be at His left, and his face will be confused, and he will say, 'The son of my son is sitting at Your right, and I am at Your left?'"[1]

In other words, Abraham is complaining to the Almighty, "How come this descendant of mine gets to sit on your right hand, and I'm only on the left?" The story assumes the verse is speaking of the Messiah and makes the point that his placement at the right hand of God makes him greater than Abraham. The text itself has King David calling the one this midrash identifies as Messiah "my Lord." So Messiah is not only greater than Abraham, but he is also greater than David, the greatest king in Israel's history.

What Mystery Is Hidden in This Psalm?

Look at how Yeshua refers to this passage in Psalm 110 to handle the continuous questioning from certain religious leaders of his day.

> While the Pharisees were gathered together, Jesus asked them a question, saying, "What do you think about the Christ? Whose Son is He?"
>
> They said to him, "The Son of David."
>
> He said to them, "How then does David in the Spirit call Him 'Lord,' saying:
>
>> 'The LORD said to my Lord,
>> "Sit at My right hand,
>> Till I make Your enemies Your footstool" '?
>
> If then David calls him 'Lord,' how is He his Son?" And no one was able to answer Him a word, nor from that day on did anyone dare question Him anymore. (Matt. 22:41–46)

Why did Yeshua pose this question? Certain rabbis who stood in opposition to Yeshua had been asking questions of him that were not so much designed to learn anything, but to see if he would incriminate himself. After answering each of their questions satisfactorily, Jesus employs their own strategy to ask a pointed question of his own, and the leaders cannot answer. The passage he quoted contained a mystery they did not want to address in his presence.

His early followers would have witnessed this confrontation and perhaps they had been pondering the question for themselves. I think it's likely that when he appeared to them to open their minds to the Scriptures, he revisited this passage with them to unpack how it is fulfilled in him. And the phrase "The LORD said to my Lord" is not the only mystery to be unpacked in Psalm 110. The passage also brings up the enigmatic concept of the Messiah's priesthood.

The Jewish Priesthood

The priesthood was an important role in Israel during Bible times, and the qualifications for that role were spelled out very clearly. In order to be a priest, you had to be from the tribe of Levi, like Moses and Aaron. And yet, one of the prophecies concerning the Messiah was that he would be from the tribe of Judah (which, of course, Jesus was). So how could the Messiah be a priest in light of this requirement?

This psalm addresses that issue: "The LORD has sworn and will not change his mind, 'You are a priest forever after the order of Melchizedek'" (Ps. 110:4 ESV). Here David references a very ambiguous figure who is mentioned just once before, in Genesis 14—a man called Melchizedek.

Who Is Melchizedek and Why Should We Care?

Melchizedek means "King of Righteousness." Most of Genesis 14 is about wars between five kings of pagan nations, including Sodom and Gomorrah, and how Lot, the nephew of Abram (before God changed his name to Abraham), was taken captive. When Abram rescued his nephew Lot, in the process he won the booty from all the kings who had ended up fleeing from the king of Sodom. But following that victory, Abram met this man who is described as king of Salem (which is a shortened name for the city of Jerusalem) as well as being the "priest of God Most High" (v. 18). Abram gave an offering to this priest, this "King of Righteousness." "And he gave him a tithe of all" (Gen. 14:20), meaning a tenth of all the booty he'd gotten from the fleeing kings (and, as an aside, Abram refused to keep the other 90 percent of the wealth for himself).

We do not know much about Melchizedek, but these few verses make a rather profound statement about him. Remember, this was before the Levitical priesthood, so if you ran across a priest, you might reasonably assume he was a pagan. Yet Abraham, father of all the Jewish people, recognized something unique about Melchizedek and honored him with a very generous tithe. So, when Psalm 110 reveals that the Messiah would be a priest forever after the order of Melchizedek, we see that he would be a priest of a very different sort. Something other than the line of Levi made Melchizedek a priest of the Most High God . . . and so it would be with the Messiah.

Melchizedek and Messiah in the Book of Hebrews

The New Testament book called "Hebrews" was written to a group of first-century Jewish believers in Jesus who were struggling to understand the full identity of Jesus as Messiah. The writer wanted them to understand that in every way, Jesus is "greater than" every other hero in biblical history.

In discussing Jesus' priesthood, the author refers back to the mention of Melchizedek from Genesis 14, as well from Psalm 110. Hebrews chapter 7 points out the connections between Jesus and this mysterious priest. It makes it clear that since Abraham paid a priestly tithe to this enigmatic character, he was honoring the priesthood of Melchizedek as greater than the Levitical priesthood that would come through Abraham's great-grandson Levi. The author of Hebrews also points out the eternal nature of Yeshua's priesthood, as seen in Psalm 110.

The Psalm 110 reference to Melchizedek confirms the priesthood of Messiah. The reference to David confirms his kingship. David was both a prophet and a king, but he was not a priest. Combine this with the reference to "a prophet like Moses" that we previously unpacked from Deuteronomy 18, and it's clear that Jesus was all three.

Why Is It Relevant That Messiah Embodies These Ancient Biblical Roles?

It's reasonable to ask how this is relevant to those of us who don't experience the roles of prophet, priest, and king as part of our everyday lives. Although these roles may seem a bit obscure in the twenty-first century, there are reasons that they were once central to Jewish life. Are you willing to ask God to open your mind to what the Bible says about the purpose of prophets, priests, and kings? Take a moment to peer into that world and see God how it relates to Yeshua, and what that might mean for our modern understanding of God.

Prophets

Although many prophecies included promises and predictions, the purpose of prophets was not to predict the future. Prophets were simply called to be God's mouthpiece. They were to deliver his messages however and to whomever God chose. This is exactly how Yeshua described himself when he said: "For I have not spoken on My own authority; but the Father who sent Me gave Me a command, what I should say and what I should speak" (John 12:49). The Messiah came as a prophet so that we could hear from God.

Priests

Jewish priests were responsible for maintaining the temple and its rituals, but the bottom line was that they served as mediators to reconcile people to God. Again, this is what Yeshua came to do. That's why he said, "I am the way, the truth, and the life. No one comes to the Father except through Me" (John 14:6).

Kings

And kings? Israel's kings were meant to be agents of God. As prophets spoke on God's behalf, so kings were meant to rule on God's behalf. Yeshua came to rule, but not in the way people expected.[2] When Pilate asked if he was King of the Jews, Yeshua was clear. He said, "You say *rightly* that I am a king. For this cause I was born, and for this cause I have come into the world, that I should bear witness to the truth. Everyone who is of the truth hears My voice" (John 18:37). But he also said, "My kingdom is not of this world" (v. 36).

Yeshua is the best of all that is good, and all that God intends for us. As our prophet Messiah, he not only speaks God's truth, he *is* God's truth. It's because Jesus is the truth that we can know and experience the love of God now and forever.

As our priestly Messiah, Yeshua intercedes for us to reconcile us to God. He is the priest *forever* because he is the Son of God who made it possible for us to share his access to the Father. No one else has given their life like he did so that we could draw close to God. No one else could. And because he rose from the dead, we know that his suffering for our salvation was not only truly loving, but truly effective.

As Messiah and King, Yeshua is the Life. Through the new covenant he established, we have a new heart, a new life to live for a merciful and loving God. It's a life that starts within us, and as we trust and obey Yeshua as King, our new inner life works its way out in the things we think, say, and do.

Conclusion

The prophecies we've explored show how God has been at work since the beginning of time. He's shone the light of his promised redemption in dark times, going all the way back to the garden of Eden. He's continued to give clues that sometimes seemed impossible and paradoxical, and yet these clues come together perfectly in the person of Yeshua.

As prophet, priest, and king, Yeshua is like no one else in history; he is greater than all. I have had many conversations with people who struggle with Jesus' claims. I often find the struggle is not necessarily because they have grounds to believe them to be untrue, but because most of us need more than a checklist or a case to prove we should follow Yeshua: we need a connection.

Like the disciples, we need help to open our minds as well as our hearts to who Yeshua is and what he's done for us. That openness allows us to realize that our spiritual lives depend on what he alone can do. That's the connection we need. Only then will we be able to accept that we cannot make a way to God; we can only take the way that he provides.

AND YOU?

The only one who can truly be our prophet, priest, and king invites us now to open our minds and open our hearts to receive all he has to give us. He is the way, the truth, and the life. He is the greatest of all time, the unique Messiah of all.

But whether or not he is the Messiah is not the only issue. The question is, do you want him to be *your* Messiah? Will you ask him to give you what you need to follow him?

More Life Stories of Minds Being Opened

Handel's Messiah Is the Jewish Messiah

As mentioned in the introduction of this book, when Ellen, a Jewish musician, attended a concert of Handel's *Messiah*, she found herself surprisingly moved. She was eager to discuss her experience with Laura Barron, a Jewish believer in Jesus who is also a colleague of mine and a longtime leader in Jews for Jesus.

"You should go hear Handel's *Messiah*," Ellen told Laura. "I think you'd like it because it's all about Jesus, based on the New Testament."

Laura smiled. "What if I told you that more than half the lyrics to that piece are from the Hebrew Scriptures?"

"But they must be from the New Testament! I know the piece is about Jesus; it was so specific and detailed."

"You're right," Laura agreed. "It *is* about Jesus, and some of the words *are* from the New Testament. But Handel's *Messiah* includes even more passages from the Jewish Bible—from Isaiah 7, Isaiah 53, Psalm 2, and Psalm 22—just to name a few!"

Ellen was astounded. Not only had it never occurred to her that the Jewish Bible would be pointing to Yeshua (Jesus), but its predictions about who the Messiah would be and what he would do were positively mind-boggling. But what, if anything, did that mean to Ellen personally? That was unclear, so Laura asked, "If you really know that Yeshua might be the promised one of Israel, what would it take for you to put your trust in him?"

"Well," Ellen threw out, almost jokingly, "I'm a music teacher and I have been looking for a job for a year. If you pray for me and I get a job . . ."

Laura prayed with her.

The next morning at 8 a.m. Ellen called to say that a Christian school had called and offered her a job. They normally only hired Christians, but someone had told the school about her.

Ellen realized that not only was Jesus the Messiah of Scripture, but he also cared about her in a real and personal way. She knew she could trust and follow him.

A Haredi Response to Isaiah 53

The word "Haredi" refers to people who belong to an especially Orthodox sect of Judaism. Jesus is considered "off-limits" in Haredi communities, and the risk of being ostracized for believing or even exploring belief in him is very real. Yet many have taken that risk, albeit very cautiously, including a man we'll call Yakov. Stephen Katz, another longtime leader on the Jews for Jesus leadership team, recalls Yakov's story.

Yakov, like most everyone in his culture, married young and had a lot of kids. He got a job in the diamond district of New York City to support his family. That's where he began questioning his religious upbringing. "I saw members of my community behaving in ways that shocked me. I saw a lot of hypocrisy when I was at work, and I didn't know what to do. I started losing my faith."

So in his crisis, Yakov goes to a book sale at Jewish Theological Seminary, which is not an Orthodox school, and is therefore avoided by Yakov's community. But at this sale, he finds a book in Yiddish and he starts reading about an amazing person who he finds really appealing. He's so drawn to this person's story that he buys the book and takes it home.

It turns out that he'd been reading a Yiddish New Testament, and the person he was drawn to was Jesus! And because he knew that Jews for Jesus had done a special outreach for his community (including sending Yiddish versions of the *Jesus* film to 25,000 Haredi homes), he contacted us. I was in New York for a month of this outreach, and I had the privilege of meeting with him.

There were not many options where Yakov and I could meet privately, but when I told him about a small Hispanic church that had opened its doors for our use, he said, "Yes, good. I'll meet you there." He suggested "meeting" at a subway stop not far from the church.

I told him what I look like and what I'd be wearing, and I figured I'd recognize him by the distinctive clothing worn by his particular community. He added, "I don't want to be seen with you, but once we spot each other, start walking to the church and I'll follow you." Sure enough, once we made eye contact, I began walking and he followed, but from across the street. Then he crossed to my side, staying a half block behind me all the way.

Our meeting went well, and it was the first of many more. One evening I opened the Hebrew Bible to Isaiah 53, handed it to him, and said, "I'd like you to read this." He starts chanting it like he's in the synagogue—chanting the whole chapter in Hebrew. And as I watch I can see the comprehension on Yakov's face. He's already been exposed to the Yiddish New Testament. He can recognize what's being written about in that passage—that it's Yeshua.

It was an incredibly powerful moment. He didn't need me to draw the connection. His mind was opening to the Scriptures—and to the one of whom they were speaking.

We met seven times over the course of the month—and when I went home to the Washington, DC, area, Yakov connected with a couple of other guys on our New York team. Eventually, he prayed to receive Yeshua as his Messiah with one of them.

A Haredi Response to the Deity of Messiah

Stephen was sharing his faith in Yeshua well before joining the staff of Jews for Jesus. Here is another of his experiences with a very Orthodox Jewish man. We don't know if he ever embraced Yeshua as Messiah, but Stephen was able to see his mind begin opening to new possibilities about the Messiah.

Fred and his wife, like many young couples in the Haredi community, had a growing family, and were eager to check out the double stroller that my wife Laura and I had advertised. We welcomed them into our apartment, and before long we struck a deal. Afterward as we were chatting, it came up that I was a Jewish believer in Yeshua.

We had a lengthy phone call shortly after that, close to two hours. Fred was adamant that the Jewish Bible nowhere suggests that the Messiah would be more than a man, which, he said, is why Jewish people don't believe in Jesus. I pulled out my Hebrew Bible, and on the other end of the phone, of course he got his.

I pointed him to Isaiah 9, and said, "Look, this child clearly is a human being because a child is being born, a son, but he's given these names, 'mighty God, wonderful counselor, Prince of Peace, everlasting father.'" And I zoomed in on the Hebrew name *El Gibor*,[1] mighty God.

Fred said, "I'm not impressed. Loads of Jewish names have the name 'El,' the name of God, in them, like Michael or Ezekiel, Daniel."

I replied, "Okay, let's turn to Jeremiah, chapter 23 verses 5 and 6." (The passage talks about the branch of David.) I said, "You know and I know that this term, the branch of David, is recognized by the rabbis as a very messianic term." Fred agreed. I continued, "So look at what Jeremiah calls him here. It says, 'and this is the name by which he [the branch of David] will be called: "the LORD is our righteousness"'" (ESV). And the word for LORD there is the ineffable name, the Tetragrammaton, which can only mean God."

I continued, "Yes, there are a lot of names that have the little piece that refers to God, but the full name of God that we don't even pronounce? There's no way a parent would name their son that, even if they act like their child hung the moon and the stars." And he agreed with that.

Finally, I said, "Look, I can't prove to you that the Messiah is God in the flesh. I can't prove that to you, Fred. But based on the verses that we've been looking at, you need to at least acknowledge that our prophets opened the door to that idea, and that from the text we've been looking at, it's possible."

There was a very, very, very long and awkward pause in the conversation on the phone. Finally, Fred said, "Yes, I see what you're saying, and that it would be possible."

A Secular Israeli Sees the New Covenant Prophesied by Jeremiah

To a secular-born Israeli like Alex Adelson, the term *brit hadasha* (*new covenant*, also translated *new testament*) was no more or less than the title of "the Christian Bible." He assumed (as many do) that it was replete with inconsistencies and traces of anti-Semitism, and that it had undergone a myriad of edits over the years. Alex says, "All these things I believed on hearsay, without ever having read it, much less researched it, for myself. And as for the notion of a 'new covenant' being rooted in the Tanakh, to me that was as paradoxical as a meat-eating vegetarian." But all that began to change when Alex heard a believer in Yeshua reciting verses from Jeremiah 31:31–34. Alex (who is now one of our long-time leaders in Israel) tells his story:

> I could hardly believe the words my friend was reciting. Could they really be from the prophet Jeremiah in the Jewish Bible? I had to know, and so I found myself poring over my own copy of the Tanakh, a token from my service in the Israeli Defense Forces.
>
> As I read, I discovered that Jeremiah, a prophet cast adrift among his exiled kin, received a message of God's enduring love and faithfulness amidst the terrible pain and suffering the prophet also describes. Forgotten though God's people may feel, God remembers them, even when they turn deaf ears to his admonitions.
>
> Despite my people's fall from grace, our abandonment of spiritual vows, God's affection remains unflinching, his willingness to absolve their transgressions steadfast. The promise of a triumphant return to Zion hangs in the air, a beacon of hope for the salvation of Israel's remnant.
>
> But I saw that God's plan, announced through the prophet Jeremiah, transcends mere geographical restoration. As I read Jeremiah, I began to understand how God yearns for a spiritual rebirth, an overhaul of our hearts. Human abilities, let alone desire to live up to God's holiness, fall short, yet he will be satisfied with no less. He longs for a relationship with us, but will not compromise the beauty of his own character.
>
> What is humanly impossible is made possible within his divine purview. Thus, he announces a new covenant. As both the architect and the guarantor of this covenant,

God promises to forgive our sins, and to etch his will and his ways onto our hearts. Only through this profound transformation will we truly live as God's people.

There, inscribed centuries before the birth of Yeshua and the authorship of the New Testament, God had prophesied a transformational covenant that I knew I had not experienced.

As I grappled with my own ignorance of Yeshua and his teachings, I was challenged to delve into the New Testament, that "forbidden book" which you will not find on the shelves of most bookstores in Israel. I found that my assumptions about the book were wrong. If you haven't read it for yourself, I would encourage you to do so. "Then you will know the truth, and the truth will set you free" (John 8:32 NIV)—and indeed, the truth revealed itself to me, and set me free to know and love God from the inside out, just as Jeremiah promised.

A Jewish Woman Asks God for a Sign

Sheila grew up in Northern Europe, raised by her Jewish parents, who are prominent in their community. As a young adult, she traveled to the US and studied at a traditionally Jewish high school. Eventually she moved to the UK, where the following story, told by my colleague Julia Pascoe in London, took place:

> When I met Sheila, she told me that she had always had a desire to know God and to know his plans for her life. Rabbinic Judaism didn't provide the answers to her deep existential questions, so she began exploring a wide

range of New Age practices and beliefs—but still, nothing satisfied her genuine desire to know God.

It wasn't until Sheila was in her late thirties that she met a Christian who dared to share the gospel with her! They spent long hours discussing the Bible, and Sheila became increasingly interested in Jesus—yet it was really difficult for her to even think about being Jewish and believing in him. She found herself wondering, "How can this be? Are there really Jews who believe that Jesus is the Messiah?" So she prayed and asked God, "If Jews really need to know Jesus, show me a sign!"

That week as she was navigating through London, she took a wrong turn, and just happened to see an enormous sign that said "Jews for Jesus." That "wrong turn" had taken her past our shop! Sheila saw that as a pretty significant sign and an answer to her prayer. She told her Christian friend about it, and the two of them came to the shop, which is where I connected with them.

Over time, Sheila and I talked about how the Jewish prophets spoke about the promised Messiah, and how Yeshua fulfilled what the prophets had said. One day as Sheila was listening to music by Joshua Aaron, she heard a song based on Jeremiah 31:31–34.

Sheila felt God softening her heart as she read his promise to put his law within her, and that he wanted to be like a husband to his people. This was very different from the teachings of the rabbis as well as the New Age religions she had dabbled in. This prophecy helped her see Jesus as Messiah from the context of her Jewish Bible.

It wasn't long before Sheila shared that she believed Jesus had died for her sins and rose from the dead. She prayed, repenting of sin, and receiving the one who would write his law in her heart. Her lifelong desire to know God and his plans for her had been met in a most unexpected way.

Messianic Prophecies "Kicked in" After He Believed in Jesus

Jeff Morgan was born and raised in a secular Jewish home in the US. At the age of twenty-four, he moved to Israel where he learned Hebrew and worked on a kibbutz. He returned to the US but over the years he made frequent trips back to Israel, where he met his wife, Yael. Wherever they made their home, he remained spiritually restless. Today Jeff and his family are believers in Yeshua, and Jeff is a vital part of our team in Israel. Here Jeff tells part of his story:

> You just can't tell from the outside what is happening in a person's heart. I was outwardly fit—in fact I was a fitness trainer. But inside I was falling apart. After twenty years of practicing New Age spirituality and meditation, I found myself depressed, hopeless, and spiritually tormented. That's when Yeshua revealed himself to my wife, my eldest son, and to me—all at the same time, but individually.
>
> Over the course of a month and a half, we heard about Jesus everywhere: from people we met, books that were handed to us, billboards, TV series, stories of radical redemption and healing, and more.
>
> One day I visited a church and heard a message from the New Testament Scriptures describing how a voice from heaven said of Yeshua, "This is my beloved son; hear him."

That's when I knew that it wasn't enough to be interested in or impressed by Yeshua. I needed to turn from my arrogant attempts to live life on my own terms and trust and follow Yeshua with all my heart. At that point God blew my heart open. He saved me from despair and gave me—and our whole family—a brand new life.

One of the ways I knew that God had made a radical change in my life was a sudden, insatiable desire I had to read the Bible. I can't say that the messianic prophecies brought me to faith in Yeshua, but without a doubt they strengthened my faith and affirmed my commitment to tell others about him.

I have a lot of great conversations with Jewish people and I continually hear: *We don't need Jesus; we have Moses.* But God knew we would need another prophet like Moses, and not only because Moses was going to die. God knew that a huge portion of the Law of Moses would one day be inapplicable along with the temple and many other aspects of life that the 613 commandments covered.

Yeshua came before the temple was destroyed. In the aftermath of that destruction, I only see two choices: we can choose to believe that oral tradition is the ultimate authority on how to live Jewishly, or we can see that Jesus is that ultimate prophet of whom Moses spoke and we can follow him.

The day when I heard the message of how God spoke from heaven telling people to hear his son, I did not realize that God confirming the promise of Deuteronomy 18. But now it is so clear to me that Moses was pointing beyond himself to the Messiah. And I know that believing in Yeshua is the most Jewish thing my family and I could do.

These are just a few examples of how people's minds are continuing to be opened to Yeshua through the Jewish Scriptures. Many more such stories are available for you to view on the Jews for Jesus YouTube channel at https://www.youtube.com/c/jewsforjesus. You can also read more at https://jewsforjesus.org/stories.

Except for Jews for Jesus staff, names are changed to protect privacy.

APPENDIX 2

Theophanies: When God Makes Appearances

A "theophany" has been defined simply as "a manifestation of God."[1] This can include anything from God's appearance in the burning bush in Exodus 3 to more human-like manifestations.

In this appendix we'll focus mainly on manifestations in human form, which tend to be somewhat mysterious and often come in the midst of dramatic stories. But we will also look at some other manifestations of God's presence.

Abraham's Three Guests (Genesis 18)

As Genesis 18 opens, we read that "the LORD appeared to him [Abraham] by the terebinth trees of Mamre" (v. 1). Right away we know that we are dealing with an appearance of God.

In the early church, many interpreted the three men as either an appearance of the Trinity, or as a pre-incarnate appearance of Jesus along with two angels. Jewish tradition, on the other hand, interpreted all three as angels. What do we actually find in Genesis 18?

In verse 2 we read that Abraham sees "three men," and that he notices their appearance very suddenly. Did Abraham not see them when they were a distance away? Commentator Gordon Wenham suggests that either Abraham had been taking a nap and suddenly woke up to find his three guests standing there, or perhaps they were supernatural beings who were capable of suddenly appearing or disappearing.

Abraham bows down to his guests in verse 2. Was this the common gesture of respect, or was it a way of showing that the visitors were more than mere human beings, for bowing was also what one did when worshiping God? Perhaps Abraham was acting "better than he knew."

Abraham addressed them, or one of them, as "my Lord" in verse 3. That was the customary way of addressing superiors, for Abraham calls himself "Your servant" and entreats them to stay as his guest for a meal. In that situation, the word for "Lord" would normally be read as *Adoni*. However, the Masoretic text (the standard edition of the Hebrew Bible) indicates the pronunciation *Adonay*, which was used in reference to God as the Lord. (In verse 1, God's personal name, *YHWH*, was used.)[2]

We read that the visitors knew Sarah's name (verse 9) without having met her, and they also knew that she laughed to herself, even though she remained unseen inside the tent.[3] It seems they are not mere men.

Then again in verse 10 God speaks. While the verse only indicates "He said," in the context it must be God who promises that Sarah will bear a son, because "He" is called YHWH in verses 13 and 14. Throughout the narrative, the text alternates between "the men" and the LORD (YHWH). To make things even more mysterious, in verse 21 the LORD (YHWH) says he will go down to Sodom to inspect the reports he has heard, while in verse 22 it is "the men" who go to Sodom, while Abraham is still there with the LORD (YHWH).

What is going on in this chapter? Is Abraham dealing with three men, or with God, or with God appearing as men, or something else? It remains unclear exactly *how* God is appearing as the three visitors.

Jewish scholar Benjamin Sommer summarized the chapter, underscoring the uncertainties that we find. (He uses "Yhwh" to indicate God by His personal name; most modern translations render this as "the LORD" or sometimes by "Yahweh.")

> Two of the visitors leave, and the one who remains with Abraham is now clearly identified as Yhwh (18.22); Abraham's knowledge is now parallel to the reader's, for in the discussion that follows it is clear that Abraham now knows who the remaining Visitor is. The other two beings are subsequently referred to as angels (*malachim*, 19.1). It is clear that Yhwh appears in bodily form to Abraham in this passage; what is less clear is whether all three bodies were Yhwh's throughout, or whether all three were Yhwh's at the outset of the chapter but only one of them by its end, or whether the other two were merely servants.[4]

Gordon Wenham attributes a purpose to these unresolved mysteries:

> Throughout these chapters, the relationships between "the LORD," "the men," and "the angels" are shrouded in mystery. . . . I see these confusions as deliberate: they express the difficulty of human comprehension of the divine world.[5]

We are invited to share with Abraham in the mystery of God's appearance to him. I see this as an enigmatic preamble to what comes much later and is presented with clarity: when God himself took on human nature in the person of Jesus.

Jacob's Wrestling Match (Genesis 32)

The future blessing of Jacob over Esau is pronounced at their birth. The actual getting of that blessing, normally given to the firstborn but taken by Jacob with the connivance of their mother, Rebekah, created a terrible rift between the two brothers.

Years later, Jacob is preparing to meet his brother Esau. When he hears that Esau is coming to meet him with four hundred men—for good or for evil, he does not know—Jacob sends his wives, children, and servants on ahead with his animals. It is within that context that we read about another blessing for Jacob in the well-known story of his wrestling match with a man who turns out to be no less than God himself. Again, it's a very mysterious passage.

In verse 24, we read the abrupt statements: "Then Jacob was left alone; and a Man wrestled with him until the breaking of day." Who is this man? Why is he wrestling with Jacob? Why doesn't Jacob stop to ask what is going on? It is as though the man appears out of nowhere and suddenly engages Jacob in a night-long wrestling match—similar to the sudden appearance of the three men in Genesis 18.

Adding to the mystery, this story is the only time that 'avaq (Hebrew "wrestle") appears in Scripture. That word sounds like the name of the stream where Jacob is camped (in Hebrew, yabboq) and also sounds like Jacob's Hebrew name itself (ya'aqov). This kind of wordplay is common in the Bible and draws attention to the who, what, and where elements of the story that sound similar.

One explanation is that Genesis takes ideas that ancient readers would have been familiar with but elevates them to the reality of the one God. For example, in pagan thought, rivers were seen as entrance points to the lands beyond, guarded by the gods. As it turns out, it is God himself, not a pagan deity, who is guarding this river, and when the wrestling match has ended and Jacob crosses the Jabbok, he indeed has entered a new land—the land of his new name as a changed man.

In addition, some ancient peoples believed that an advantage could be gained by holding onto a god; in one pagan story, the "god" invites a king to prevail over him in order to secure a blessing. Genesis turns this idea into the reality that Jacob held onto "the man" until he was finally blessed.

Seemingly, this man could have won the match at any time (since, by a simple touch, he could put out Jacob's hip, v. 25). Yet the same verse says he inflicted the injury "when He saw that He did not prevail against him." Finally, in verse 26, the man tells Jacob to let him go, "for the day breaks." Remember, this was a nighttime wrestling match. Perhaps he does not wish to be seen by Jacob—for if he is God, then as we later read in Exodus 33:20, "You cannot see My face; for no man shall see Me, and live." Jacob, however, refuses to release the man until he receives his blessing.

Then comes the matter of names. The man asks for Jacob's name, and hearing the response, gives him the new name of "Israel," meaning "striver," for "you have struggled with God and with men, and have prevailed" (v. 28). In return Jacob asks for the man's name, but he only replies, "Why is it that you ask about My name?" This is reminiscent of a verse in the book of Judges, when Samson's father asks after the angel's name, not realizing who he was, and the reply is, "Why do you ask My name, seeing it is wonderful?" (Judg. 13:18). The word *wonderful* is related to the name "Wonderful, Counselor" in Isaiah 9:6, and is nearly always used in connection with God.

Jacob realizes that something is truly out of the ordinary. He names the place where they wrestled "Peniel," which means "face of God," and he explains, "For I have see God face to face, and my life is preserved" (Gen. 32:30). Of course, he did not actually see God's face, but the face of God appearing as a man, and he was certainly up close and personal as they wrestled.

As in the Genesis 18 passage, readers may wonder: was the man an appearance of the pre-incarnate Jesus? And as with Genesis 18, early Christian writers were divided in their opinion, some saying that this was God the Father and others, God the Son. It may be best not to try to parse that out but to simply recognize the mystery and miracle of God's awe-inspiring appearance to Jacob. From that encounter, Jacob received a blessing, and one far better than the one he received from Isaac. For this encounter changed not only Jacob's name, but his character, and hence his destiny.

But there is more. This interpretation finds confirmation in Hosea 12:4–5 ESV, which speaks of this very incident in poetic form. Jacob, says Hosea,

> strove with the angel and prevailed;
> he wept and sought his favor.
> He met God at Bethel,
> and there God spoke with us—
> the LORD, the God of hosts,
> the LORD is his memorial name.

Despite some difficulties in interpreting this passage, Benjamin Sommer writes:

> In other words, in Hosea 12 the being who wrestled with Jacob . . . was the God Yhwh. . . . The reason for the apparent

confusion between God and angel in these verses from Hosea is simply that both passages, Hosea 12 and Genesis 32, reflect a belief that the selves of an angel and the God Yhwh could overlap or that a small-scale manifestation or fragment of Yhwh can be termed a *mal'akh* [angel].[4]

Though "fragments" of God may be an unusual way of putting it, Sommer's point is that Jacob's opponent at the Jabbok ford was no less than God himself, manifesting in human form—in fact, not simply *appearing human* as in a vision, but as an *actual human being* who could touch Jacob and physically wrestle with him. With Jacob, as with Abraham, we encounter the mystery of God's being, and an echo of the later incarnation that would take place in the person of Jesus.

The Angel of the LORD

The above two passages stand out for their uniqueness and the sense of mystery about God that they impart. They are "one-off" occurrences. But in Scripture, we also find a recurring character known most frequently as "the Angel of the LORD."

Earlier we referred to the story of Samson's parents, found in Judges 13. Let's take a closer look. In verse 3, the "Angel of the LORD" appears to Samson's unnamed mother. He gives her a promise of a son (Samson) to be born to her as well as instructions as to how she should raise him. But when she reports the incident to her husband, Manoah, she only says: "A man of God came to me, and his appearance was like the appearance of the angel of God, very awesome. I did not ask him where he was from, and he did not tell me his name" (v. 6 ESV).

She calls him "a man of God," which is an expression used elsewhere for human prophets (Deut. 33:1; 1 Sam. 2:27; 9:6; 1

Kings 12:22). She says he looks like "the angel of God" but she seems to believe him to be no more than a human being. In verse 8 Manoah seems to believe the same, for he prays to God to send "the Man of God." Yet in verse 9 we read that the "the Angel of God" came back to Samson's mother for another visit.

In fact, the text oscillates between calling this person "the man" and "the angel of the LORD." Yet as far in the narrative as verse 16, Manoah is unaware of anything out of the ordinary.

And then comes verse 17, where the matter of the name of the visitor resurfaces, as it did in Genesis 32. As noted above, the man simply replies that his name is "wonderful," a term used elsewhere in connection with God. This is indeed a hint that the visitor is more than merely human, but Manoah and his wife still don't perceive that—until the climax of the story.

That climax comes in verses 19–21 when the couple makes an offering of a goat. The narrator remarks that they make it "to the LORD, to the one who works wonders" (ESV). The word *wonders* is closely related to the word *wonderful* in the previous verse. It is as if the narrator is cluing the readers in as to the identity of the "man"—but Manoah and his wife *still* do not know.

All that changes in verse 20, when the "angel of the LORD" goes up into the altar's flames and disappears. Manoah finally recognizes that it is the angel of the LORD (v. 21). He realizes that this was an appearance of God himself, for in verse 22, he says, "We shall surely die, because we have seen God." It must have sent a chill up Manoah's spine to be speaking one moment to someone whom he thought was just a "man," and then to see him ascend in the smoke and fire of the offering—and realize it had been God himself all along! His wife calms him down and assures him that it was not God's intention to kill them.

So is this being a man, an angel, or God? Once again, we see that God appears in human form, or in angelic form, or somehow as both. Indeed, the mystery of the "angel of the LORD" is that he is "a heavenly being sent by God to deal with men as his personal agent and spokesman."[6] And yet he is often "virtually identified with God and speaks not merely in the name of God but as God in the first person singular."[7]

We can see this Angel of the LORD speaking as God in Genesis 16, where he encounters Hagar as she flees from her mistress Sarah. At one point, this angel tells Hagar, "I will surely multiply your offspring so that they cannot be numbered for multitude" (Gen. 16:10 ESV), echoing the earlier promise that God himself had made to Abraham. Indeed, it is a promise that only God could make. Likewise, in Genesis 21:18, the same angel reappears to Hagar and announces concerning Ishmael, "I will make him a great nation." Once again, this is a promise only God can accomplish, and which he earlier made to Abraham.

And then there is the story of the near-sacrifice of Isaac in Genesis 22, known in Jewish tradition as the *Akedah* (binding), which we discuss in Appendix 3. Here God calls to Abraham in verse 1, yet it is the angel of the Lord who repeats that same call in verse 11. Moreover, in verse 12, the angel says "now I know that you fear God" (as though speaking of God as someone else) and immediately adds, "you have not withheld your son, your only son, from Me." The *me* can be none other than God himself.

The Jewish Bible gives many instances where people encounter a being who at one moment seems to be an angel, at another moment God himself, or perhaps both simultaneously. G. H. Twelftree notes that in these encounters, we find a "living portrayal of an encounter with God, which because of the dangers of an immediate theophany was also understood as having been mediated in some way."[8] In other words, God appeared in these ways because no one could survive a direct encounter with Him.

He therefore appeared as men, as angels, or even in other forms, as we will now see.

God's Appearances in Other Forms

God first appeared to Moses not as a man or an angel, but as a fire that roared through a desert bush yet never consumed the bush.[9] During the wilderness wanderings, God went before Israel as a pillar of fire during the night and as a column of smoke by day. Exodus 13:21 (ESV) remarks that this was God himself going before the people: "And the LORD went before them by day in a pillar of cloud to lead them along the way, and by night in a pillar of fire to give them light, that they might travel by day and by night." And yet Exodus 14:19 says that it is the angel of God (another name for the angel of the LORD) who was traveling with them in the form of fire and cloud! So God/the angel of the LORD/the angel of God appeared not only in human form but as fire and cloud as well.

Certain appearances of the Lord take the form of God's visible glory. In Exodus 16:7, 10, Moses told the people that they would "see the glory of the LORD" when he provided manna to eat from heaven. This was not just a way of saying that they would see God take action to feed them. For in verse 10, the people "looked toward the wilderness, and behold, the glory of the LORD appeared in the cloud." This was a *visible* appearance of God. Just as he appeared as a man and as an angel, he appeared now in a cloud.

In Exodus 19:18, God's personal presence again took the form of fire: "Now Mount Sinai was completely in smoke because the LORD had descended upon it in fire." Similarly Exodus 24:17 (ESV) describes the appearance of God: "Now the appearance of the glory of the LORD was like a devouring fire on the top of the mountain in the sight of the people of Israel."

We find a unique description of God's presence in the tabernacle in Exodus 40. After telling us that "Moses finished the work" of constructing the tabernacle, Scripture tells us, "Then the cloud covered the tent of meeting, and the glory of the LORD filled the tabernacle." Not only that, but "Moses was not able to enter the tabernacle of meeting, because the cloud rested above it, and the glory of the LORD filled the tabernacle" (Ex. 40:35). This is the same Moses who had met with God on Mount Sinai! It is unclear if Moses could not enter the tabernacle because the cloud obscured his vision, or because God's glory was overwhelming—perhaps it was both.

Eventually the tabernacle was replaced by the temple that King Solomon built, and just as with the earlier tabernacle, the visible glory of the Lord settled within it: "And when the priests came out of the Holy Place, a cloud filled the house of the LORD, so that the priests could not stand to minister because of the cloud, for the glory of the LORD filled the house of the LORD" (1 Kings 8:10–11 ESV).

In later Judaism, the visible manifestation of God's glory was called the *shekhinah*, from the word "to dwell"—because God's glory dwelt in the tabernacle and temple.

Many years later, when God became man in the person of Jesus, we read that "the Word became flesh and dwelt among us, and we have seen his glory, glory as of the only Son from the Father, full of grace and truth" (John 1:14 ESV).

In Jesus we see the fullness of both deity and humanity in a way the earlier theophanies could never do, for Jesus became the dwelling place—the tabernacle, the temple—of God on earth. All the appearances of God in the Old Testament were mysterious hints and glimpses of the future incarnation.

Types: Pictures of Messiah in the Jewish Bible

What Is a Type?

In everyday language, a *type* is a kind of something: maples are a type of tree; spaniels are a type of dog; nonfiction is a type of book.

In biblical studies, the word *type* is used differently. It refers to a person, or a place, or really anything else, that serves as an analogy to picture or point to something that comes later in the Bible.

These types provide patterns in Scripture. Many people or events in the Old Testament become pictures or analogies for people or events in the New Testament.

Typology is the word that refers to this kind of biblical analogy. Biblical scholar Chris Wright explains,

We have seen how the Old Testament itself has a kind of internal typology. . . . *Sodom and Gomorrah* become proverbial for God's judgment against human sin. . . . The *exodus* is repeatedly used as a model for subsequent historical acts of deliverance. Even individuals can take on this "typical" dimension—*David*, of course, as the ideal king, but also *Abraham* as the model of faith and obedience (Gen. 15:6), and *Moses* as the model prophet (Deut. 18:15, 18). So the use of "types" in the sense of examples or models is commonly found within the Old Testament.[1]

We see the use of such analogies within the Old Testament itself as well as in rabbinic tradition, but for the purpose of this book, we are focused on types from the Jewish Bible that point to Yeshua as Messiah.[2]

Passover and the Exodus

Reference: Exodus 12
Fulfillment: Various New Testament passages, see below

There may be no image of redemption more central in Scripture than the story of Passover and the Exodus from Egypt, recounted every year at the Passover *seder*. The book of Exodus relates how four hundred years of Israelite slavery were ended, beginning with God's call of Moses at the burning bush, followed by a series of highly dramatic encounters with Pharaoh, including God's visitation of the Ten Plagues upon Egypt.

The tenth and final plague was the death of the firstborn. Although the people of Israel had not been subjected to several of the other plagues, with the tenth plague came special instructions that would be necessary for them to be spared. On the night the plague struck, they were to kill a lamb and put its blood on the doorposts of their homes. The plague of death would pass over (spare) those who were safely within homes that were marked by the blood.

Following this final plague, the Exodus became a reality as Israel was liberated from their taskmasters. This familiar story is reflected in in the life of Jesus in the New Testament.

Jesus Referred to as the Lamb

In John 1:29, the person known as John the Baptist (or Baptizer) says: "Behold! The Lamb of God who takes away the sin of the world!" A day later, John repeated this (John 1:36): "And looking at Jesus as He walked, he said, 'Behold the Lamb of God!'"

The image of a lamb could point to several things: the blood of the Passover lamb that spared Israel from death; the lamb that was eaten each year at Passover in remembrance of that very first Passover; and the lambs that were daily sacrificed in the Temple to atone for sin (and for other purposes). John may have been thinking of all of these things, but the rest of his gospel gives us a clue why he called Jesus the Lamb of God.

John depicts Jesus as being crucified at the time the Passover lambs were being sacrificed in the Temple.[3] He notes in 19:33 that the soldiers did not break his legs. This, John says, "fulfilled" the Scripture about not breaking the bones of the Passover lamb (v. 36; Ex. 12:46; Num. 9:12). The Passover lamb becomes a *type*, a picture, of Jesus. Just as the blood of the lamb on the first Passover in Egypt spared Israel from death, so also Jesus' death as our Passover Lamb spares us from the deadly results of our sins.

Jesus' "Last Supper" Was a Passover Meal

While John focuses on who Jesus *was* (the Passover lamb), the other three gospels focus on what Jesus *did* at Passover. They describe the Last Supper in some detail as a sort of "version 1.0" of today's annual Passover *seder*.[4]

At this meal held with his disciples, we see the unleavened bread, or *matzah* (Luke 22:19; Ex. 12:18); the dip, probably the bitter herbs or *maror* (Mark 14:20; Ex. 12:8); and the cups (of wine; Luke 22:17, 20—these were a later tradition not found in the Old Testament). Of special interest is what Jesus said over the bread and the wine in Luke 22:19–20:

> And He took bread, gave thanks and broke it, and gave it to them, saying, "This is My body which is given for you; do this in remembrance of Me." Likewise He also took the cup after supper, saying, "This cup is the new covenant in My blood, which is shed for you."

Matthew is more explicit about the meaning of the cup: "Then He took the cup, and gave thanks, and gave it to them, saying, 'Drink from it, all of you. For this is My blood of the new covenant, which is shed for many for the remission of sins'" (Matt. 26:27–28). Jesus, then, spoke about the matzah and wine as referring to his own body and blood, which he connected with his atoning death for the forgiveness of sins. It's interesting that in some Jewish traditions, the wine is supposed to be red to remind us of the blood of the Passover lamb.[5]

In making this connection at Passover, Jesus was speaking of another redemption soon to occur: not the deliverance from Egypt, but deliverance from sin and death through his atoning sacrifice. The Passover meal was a picture or *type* of the redemption Jesus brought.

Of course Passover and the Exodus were not *merely* patterns for the future. God used those historic events to establish his people Israel. As such, the original Passover and Exodus remain a source of identity for contemporary Jewish people to remember every year, as well as offering vital teaching for the church. What God did in history came to its fulfillment in Jesus the Messiah, but those acts of God retain in themselves powerful lessons on God, his power, his faithfulness in fulfilling his promises, and much more.

The Serpent

Reference

> Then the LORD said to Moses, "Make a fiery serpent, and set it on a pole; and it shall be that everyone who is bitten, when he looks at it, shall live." So Moses made a bronze serpent, and put it on a pole; and so it was, if a serpent had bitten anyone, when he looked at the bronze serpent, he lived. (Num. 21:8–9)

Fulfillment

> And as Moses lifted up the serpent in the wilderness, even so must the Son of Man be lifted up, that whoever believes in Him should not perish but have eternal life. (John 3:14–15)

In the book of Numbers, God sent a plague of "fiery" or poisonous snakes (the word "poisonous" could also mean "burning") to judge the Israelites for rebelling against him and against Moses. The people confessed their sin and asked Moses to intercede so that God would end the plague. Moses did so, and God prescribed the remedy. The Israelites were to look at a bronze (or copper) serpent constructed by Moses in order to live.

At first this episode seems strange and rather arbitrary in its focus on snakes. Why snakes? And why a bronze image of a snake? But the episode actually makes sense in light of the fact that Israel had been living in Egypt for several centuries. Snakes were prominent in Egyptian religion and were considered to be dangerous powers on one hand, but also powers that offered protection on the other. The venomous snakes brought destruction to Israel, while in contrast the bronze serpent offered them protection.

Moreover, in ancient societies it was commonly believed that images could serve as protection against the very things they represented. (That idea is found in 1 Samuel 6, where the Philistines make gold images of rats and tumors to ward off the real rats and tumors God had sent among them.) We can see how God used the cultural context that the Israelites had been used to after living for centuries in Egypt as a vehicle of their salvation. God communicates through what is familiar—what is either known or believed—to help people grasp something previously unknown.

But there was a crucial difference between God's remedy and the Egyptian religion. For Israel, this was a matter of faith, not magic or manipulation. There was nothing automatic about just letting your eyes land on the bronze serpent. In fact, two different words are used in verses 8 and 9 of Numbers 21 for "looking." The word in verse 9, *habet*, may carry overtones of paying attention, understanding, fixing one's gaze.

Jewish tradition is also explicit that it was not the bronze serpent itself that saved the Israelites, but God, when approached in faith, who saved the people. The Mishnah (from the second century AD) comments on this incident:

> Similarly, you can say: "Make for yourself a fiery serpent, and set it upon a pole; and it shall come to pass, that everyone that is bitten, when he sees it, he shall live." Did the serpent kill, or did the serpent preserve life? Rather,

when the Jewish people turned their eyes upward and subjected their hearts to their Father in Heaven, they were healed, but if not, they rotted.[6]

Jesus used this image of the serpent being lifted up to point to what he was about to suffer, and why: "And as Moses lifted up the serpent in the wilderness, even so must the Son of Man be lifted up, that whoever believes in Him should not perish but have eternal life" (John 3:14–15). The "Son of Man" is Jesus' favorite title for himself, and here he speaks of being "lifted up" as the bronze serpent was lifted up. John's gospel uses the expression "lifted up" also in 8:28 and 12:32 to indicate his crucifixion (being lifted up on the cross) as well as his exaltation (being lifted up to heaven). The idea is that by fixing our eyes in faith on Jesus, we receive eternal life, rather than condemnation and death. Indeed, the "plague" from which we are rescued is that of death. These verses also bring to mind Isaiah 52:13, where the Servant of the Lord is "exalted" and "extolled." As the fulfillment of that passage also, Jesus is the Servant of the Lord whose death and whose being "lifted up" in exaltation heal us and give us life. In these ways the bronze serpent was a *type* of the salvation we receive in Jesus.

Water from the Rock

Reference

> "Behold, I will stand before you there on the rock in Horeb; and you shall strike the rock, and water will come out of it, that the people may drink." And Moses did so in the sight of the elders of Israel. (Ex. 17:6)

> And Moses and Aaron gathered the assembly together before the rock; and he said to them, "Hear now, you rebels!

Must we bring water for you out of this rock?" Then Moses lifted his hand and struck the rock twice with his rod; and water came out abundantly, and the congregation and their animals drank. (Num. 20:10–11)

Fulfillment:

Moreover, brethren, I do not want you to be unaware that all our fathers were under the cloud, all passed through the sea, all were baptized into Moses in the cloud and in the sea, all ate the same spiritual food, and all drank the same spiritual drink. For they drank of that spiritual Rock that followed them, and that Rock was [Messiah].[7] (1 Cor. 10:1–4)

Clearly Paul is writing about the Jewish experiences as recorded in Exodus and Numbers. When Israel was redeemed from Egypt, God led them through the Red Sea.[8] He then guided them with his own presence in a pillar of cloud during the day and a pillar of fire at night. He gave them manna to eat in the wilderness, and water to drink from a rock, which issued forth when Moses struck it with his rod. Besides physical food and drink, they received spiritual nourishment from God's presence and from the leadership of Moses.

Two things in the Hebrew Scriptures help explain what Paul is saying:

1. God is frequently called a "rock" in Scripture. (Numerous references to this include Deut. 32:4, 15, 18; 2 Sam. 22:47; 23:3; Ps. 89:26; 94:22; 95:1; Isa. 17:10). Drawing from Psalms, Jewish liturgy uses this imagery in a refrain, commonly recited in synagogue services: "Let the words of my mouth and the meditation of my heart be acceptable in your sight, O LORD, my rock and my redeemer" (Ps. 19:14 ESV).

2. The two incidents with water from the rock occur at the start and near the end of the wilderness journey. This suggests that God's provision lasted from start to finish of the forty-year journey.

That latter of the two points may be the reason for an idea that developed in Jewish tradition, namely, that the source of water actually followed the Israelites through the wilderness for forty years!

So in what way was the water from the rock a "type" of Jesus? Here is the relevant passage from the New Testament:

> Moreover, brethren, I do not want you to be unaware that all our fathers were under the cloud, all passed through the sea, all were baptized into Moses in the cloud and in the sea, all ate the same spiritual food, and all drank the same spiritual drink. For they drank of that spiritual Rock that followed them, and that Rock was [Messiah].[9] (1 Cor. 10:1–4)

First, Paul describes the experience of the Israelites as being "baptized" into Moses. By passing through the sea and experiencing what God did for them in the wilderness, Israel was initiated into a new way of life involving Moses' leadership and the Law—just as water baptism initiates believers in Jesus, and just as proselyte baptism initiates a convert to Judaism. So, the point is that Israel began a new way of life altogether when they came out of Egypt.

Second, Paul seems to pick up on some of the traditions involving the source of water "following" Israel in the wilderness. However, he changes things from a literal rock (or well, or stream) following Israel into a "spiritual" rock. In other words, God's provision was more than just physical, and that provision came from God, Israel's "Rock" (see the Old Testament references above), who accompanied Israel for the forty years in the wilderness. In this way Paul connects with readers who may have known of the tradition—a helpful way to communicate—and tells them that it was actually the Messiah himself who provided for Israel.

Third, by linking Jesus to the "Rock," he uses a term used for the God of Israel. In this way he seems to be equating the Messiah Jesus with God. Paul applies terms used for God in the Old Testament directly to Jesus in other letters as well.

Paul shows us, then, that Jesus the Messiah was the one who provided for Israel in the wilderness as he provides for us today. He is our Rock, the God of Israel incarnate.

The *Akedah*

Reference

> Now it came to pass after these things that God tested Abraham, and said to him, "Abraham!" And he said, "Here I am." Then He said, "Take now your son, your only son Isaac, whom you love, and go to the land of Moriah, and offer him there as a burnt offering on one of the mountains of which I shall tell you." (Gen. 22:1–2)

Fulfillment

> For God so loved the world that He gave His only begotten Son, that whoever believes in Him should not perish but have everlasting life. (John 3:16)

Genesis 22 is one of the strangest stories in Scripture.[10] Most of the chapter is taken up with the *Akedah*, the story of the binding of Isaac. This portion is read every year in the synagogue on Rosh Hashanah and has been the topic of innumerable sermons, thought pieces, and discussions.

174

The *Akedah* recounts how God called to Abraham and gave him this unfathomable command: "Take now your son, your only son Isaac, whom you love, and go to the land of Moriah, and offer him there as a burnt offering on one of the mountains of which I shall tell you" (Gen. 22:2). It is especially strange because the Bible forbids human sacrifice. Nevertheless, Abraham takes Isaac, goes up the mountain, binds Isaac on the altar, raises the knife to slay his son, and is only stopped when the Angel of the Lord cries out, "Do not lay your hand on the lad, or do anything to him; for now I know that you fear God, since you have not withheld your son, your only son, from Me" (v. 12). As Abraham looks up, he sees a ram in the bushes, and it becomes the actual sacrifice in place of Isaac.

Clues that all may not be as it first seems are scattered throughout this chapter. En route, Abraham tells his servants, "Stay here with the donkey; the lad and I will go yonder and worship, and we will come back to you" (Gen. 22:5). Was that a ruse or did Abraham know something? Then, when Isaac wonders why there is no lamb for the burnt offering, his father tells him, "My son, God will provide for Himself the lamb for a burnt offering" (Gen. 22:8). Again: was that an evasion, or a genuine hope?

Jewish tradition is not silent about the meaning of the *Akedah*. One of the most intriguing interpretations sees the sacrifice as actually having been consummated, and as effecting atonement for Israel in the same manner as animal sacrifices. Writes W. Gunther Plaut:

> There was . . . a remarkable tradition that insisted that Abraham completed the sacrifice and that afterward Isaac was miraculously revived. . . . According to this haggadah, Abraham slew his son, burnt his victim, and the ashes

remain as a stored-up merit and atonement for Israel in all generations.[11]

How did such a tradition get started, especially when the Genesis account specifically tells us that Isaac did *not* die? Some surmise that it arose in reaction to Christian teaching, to show that the sacrifice of Isaac was not less effective than that of Jesus; the parallel between these stories and the death and resurrection of Jesus is obvious. We also see this parallel in the work of a famous Jewish artist.

The famous twentieth-century Russian-French Jewish artist Marc Chagall painted many biblical scenes, among other themes. In some of his most well-known paintings he portrays Jesus on the cross as a symbol of Jewish suffering and martyrdom. Jesus appears also in Chagall's painting *The Sacrifice of Isaac*. The painting is readily available to see online.

In *The Sacrifice of Isaac*, we see Isaac in yellow, bound on the altar. There stands Abraham, in red, the knife raised to perform the sacrifice of his son. In blue, the angel of the Lord is stopping him, while on the left we see the ram caught in the bushes and, though she is not mentioned in Genesis 22, Abraham's wife Sarah looking on. And finally, at the top right is a scene of Jesus carrying his cross, the color red dripping down onto Abraham, suggestive of blood.

Like Genesis 22 itself, Chagall's painting encourages discussion and maybe even multiple interpretations. Chagall did not believe Jesus to be the Messiah, but he was fascinated with him as a symbol for the suffering of the Jewish people. In his own way, he connected Jesus to the story we read each Rosh Hashanah. Was he aware that there is correspondence between Genesis and, of all things, John's gospel in the New Testament?

Recall that in Genesis 22:2, God told Abraham: "Take now your son, your only son Isaac, whom you love." In John 3:16—possibly the most famous verse in the New Testament—we read: "For God so loved the world that He gave His only begotten Son, that whoever believes in Him should not perish but have everlasting life."

The connection is clear. As a Jewish author, surely John had the *Akedah* in mind. Just as Abraham loved God enough that he was willing to offer up his only son, so God loved us enough to do the same. And what about Isaac? Was it because he too loved God and his father that he did not complain, but willingly went to the altar?

Jesus willingly offered his life too: "Therefore My Father loves Me, because I lay down My life that I may take it again. No one takes it from Me, but I lay it down of Myself" (John 10:17–18).

There are other echoes of the *Akedah* in the New Testament. Paul, in his letter to the congregation in Rome, which consisted of both Jewish and Gentile followers of Yeshua, wrote: "He who did not spare His own Son, but delivered Him up for us all, how shall He not with Him also freely give us all things?" (Rom. 8:32).

And so, the *Akedah* is a picture of God who, like Abraham, offers his beloved son. It is also a picture of Yeshua, who, like Isaac, willingly goes along to his death; and, as reflected in Jewish midrash, of Yeshua who rose from the dead even as Isaac in the midrash rose from death.

Acknowledgments

This book has been shaped by multiple influences and experiences—including some that directly opposed my faith. In fact, as a Jewish believer in Jesus, I've learned almost as much from people who've disputed my beliefs as I have from those who share them. I enjoy engaging with skeptics, seekers, and believers alike. Regardless of which group best describes you, I pray that these pages spoke to you about Jesus in a new way.

My desire to write this book was fueled by a lifetime love for studying the Jewish Bible combined with decades of sharing what I have learned with others. Many people have had a key part of the process of bringing it all together. I am grateful for the opportunity I had to develop and teach portions of this book at my home congregation, Cornerstone in San Francisco. Then came the refining and sharpening push and pull of collaboration with Ruth Rosen, my dear friend and trusty editor for more than three decades. Dr. Richard Robinson, our Senior Researcher at Jews for Jesus, and another dear friend for nearly as long—is also part of my "iron sharpens iron" team.

I am eternally grateful to my wife, Sabra, and my children, Isaac, Shaina, Ilana, and Sivan as well as my grandchildren, Norah,

Levy, and Itai. Their love and support lifted and energized me through a hectic schedule, and their patience gave me permission to keep working on this book even while we were on vacations together. Thanks family!

Most of all, I am grateful to the God of Abraham, Isaac, and Jacob for sending us His Messiah, Yeshua, through whom we can have purpose and peace that passes understanding in this life, and complete forgiveness and joy for all eternity!

Notes

Introduction: Opened Minds Open Up Possibilities

1. Ellen's story is continued in Appendix 1.

2. A similar phrase, "that the Scriptures might be fulfilled," occurs throughout the eyewitness accounts of Jesus' life and mission as recorded in the New Testament. But it was not until Jesus opened their minds that his disciples were able to make (and write about) the connection. If you ask, he will make the connection for you as well.

3. The Luke 24 passage is one of several New Testament passages that document his post-crucifixion appearances over a period of forty days. For more about the New Testament as a reliable source document, consider Paul Barnett, *Is the New Testament Reliable?*, 2nd ed. (Downers Grove, IL: InterVarsity Press, 2004) or Craig Blomberg, *The Historical Reliability of the New Testament: Countering the Challenges to Evangelical Christian Beliefs* (Nashville: B&H Academic, 2016).

Chapter 1: Why a Messiah?

1. The NKJV has "bruise" and "bruise," while NIV has "crush" and "strike." The same Hebrew word is used both for what the serpent does and what the seed of the woman does.

2. Some interpret the contrast between crushing the head and bruising the heel as indicating a lethal blow and a non-lethal blow respectively. But certainly a snakebite to the heel could be lethal as well. The medieval Jewish commentator Rashi argued that the wound inflicted by the serpent is equally as lethal as the wound inflicted on him, for, he asked, where else can a snake strike, anyway? Both views present valid ways of understanding the bruised heel. If, as we believe, this individual is Jesus, whether or not the bruised heel depicts a mortal blow, his resurrection renders it ultimately non-lethal.

3. *Targum Pseudo-Jonathan*, cited in Samson H. Levey, *The Messiah: An Aramaic Interpretation: The Messianic Exegesis of the Targum* (Cincinnati: Hebrew Union College - Jewish Institute of Religion, 1974). Even more explicitly, *Genesis Rabbah* tells us, "R. Tanḥuma said in the name of Samuel Kozith: (She hinted at) that seed which would arise from another source, viz. the king Messiah."

Chapter 2: Get Out . . . and Be Blessed!

1. For Jewish interpretations, see, e.g., https://www.jtsa.edu/torah/the-tower-of-babel/; https://www.chabad.org/library/article_cdo/aid/1013006/jewish/The-Tower-of-Babel-What-Was-Up-With-lt.htm; https://www.jewishvirtuallibrary.org/tower-of-babel.

Chapter 3: Member of the Tribe

1. Various targumim (Pseudo-Jonathan; Onkelos; Fragmentary); *Sanhedrin* 98b; Rashi on Genesis 49.

Chapter 6: A Big Deal over a Little Town

1. *Emmanuel* is an alternate spelling for *Immanuel.*
2. Babylonian Talmud, *Rosh Hashanah* 25a.
3. Jerusalem Talmud *Berachot* 2:4, cited in Peter Schäfer, *The Jewish Jesus: How Judaism and Christianity Shaped Each Other* (Princeton, NJ: Princeton University Press, 2012), Kindle edition location 3233.
4. Micah 5:1 in the Jewish translation. See Michael A. Rydelnik, "The Old Testament in the New Testament," in *The Moody Handbook of Messianic Prophecy: Studies and Expositions of the Messiah in the Old Testament*, ed. Michael Rydelnik and Edwin Blum (Chicago: Moody, 2019), Kindle edition p. 105. Interestingly, the medieval midrash *Pirkei DeRabbi Eliezer* suggests the same: "Another verse says, 'But thou, Bethlehem Ephrathah, which art to be least among the thousands of Judah, from thee shall he come forth unto me who is to be ruler over Israel; whose ancestry belongs to the *past*, even to the days of old' (Mic. 5:2). 'The past,' whilst as yet the world had not been created." Cited from https://www.sefaria.org/Pirkei_DeRabbi_Eliezer.3?lang=bi.
5. For example, Targum Jonathan, as cited in Samson H. Levey, *The Messiah: An Aramaic Interpretation: The Messianic Exegesis of the Targum* (Cincinnati: Hebrew Union College - Jewish Institute of Religion, 1974), 92. See also *Pirkei DeRabbi Eliezer* 3:4, https://www.sefaria.org/Pirkei_DeRabbi_Eliezer.3.4?lang=bi.

Chapter 7: The Dilemma of the Missing Prophecy

1. "Because of the Christological interpretation given to the chapter by Christians, it is omitted from the series of prophetical lessons (Haftarot) of the Deuteronomy Sabbaths. These seven lessons are called the 'Seven (Chapters) of

Comfort' and are taken from the preceding and following parts of the book: the omission is deliberate and striking. (H. L.)." In *A Rabbinic Anthology*, ed. C. G. Montefiore and H. Loewe (New York: Schocken Books, 1974), 544.

2. Dominick S. Hernández, *Engaging the Old Testament: How to Read Biblical Narrative, Poetry, and Prophecy Well* (Grand Rapids: Baker Academic, 2023), 268–70.

3. In Bible times, God accepted the offering of an innocent animal as an atonement for sin; however, once Messiah came to offer final and full atonement, the animal sacrifices that foreshadowed him were no longer necessary. See appendix 3 on p. 169.

4. "If we do not repent, the events of Ben Joseph will come to pass. But if we repent, they will not, and Messiah ben David will appear to us suddenly. And if Messiah ben Joseph precedes him he will be as a messenger of Messiah ben David, as one who prepares the nation and clears the road of stones . . . and as one who cleanses in fire those guilty of great sins, and as one who washes with lye those guilty of small sins. . . ." In Raphael Patai, *The Messiah Texts: Jewish Legends of Three Thousand Years* (Detroit: Wayne State University Press, 1988), Kindle edition location 6239.

Chapter 8: An Ancient Clue About What's New

1. Alon Goshen-Gottstein, "The New Covenant—Jeremiah 31:30-33 (31:31-34) in Jewish Interpretation," *Studies in Christian-Jewish Relations* 15, no. 1 (2020): 1–31. Goshen-Gottstein is referring to the *Musaf* service for Yom Kippur, in the section, "The Avodah Service." The Hebrew text can be found at https://www.sefaria.org/Machzor_Yom_Kippur_Ashkenaz%2C_Musaf_for_Yom_Kippur%2C_The_Avodah_Service.66?vhe=The_Metsudah_Machzor._Metsudah_

Publications,_New_York_-_Heb_(paragraph_ed.)&lang=bi&
with=all&lang2=en).

2. In Goshen-Gottstein's words, "These liturgical expressions demonstrate how the prophecy is taken up in religious imagination, unencumbered by additional burdens, polemical, philosophical or otherwise. It remains a promise to look to, a hope for the future, a way of reconfiguring the relationship that offers a new bright future for the relationship." (Ibid.)

3. Ibid.

4. Some promises concerning Messiah remain to be fulfilled, specifically those that describe events that will come in what's often called "the end times," but that is a subject for another book!

Chapter 9: King Messiah, God's Own Son

1. From *Yalkut Shimoni* on Nach 620, par. 3, at https://www .sefaria.org/Yalkut_Shimoni_on_Nach.620.3?lang=bi.

Chapter 10: Hope Beyond the Grave

1. Although the word *resurrection* is not used in the Hebrew Scriptures, the concept is implied in passages like Daniel 12:2. The resurrection is part of Maimonides' Thirteen Principles of Faith, which is recited by many Orthodox Jewish people to this day.

2. Hannah also anticipated the coming of that Hasid (1 Sam. 2:9–10), as did a later psalmist (Ps. 89:19–20 [vv. 20–21 in the Hebrew Bible]).

Chapter 11: Famous Last Words

1. He was speaking Aramaic (a language related to Hebrew).

Chapter 12: Messiah the GOAT

1. *Midrash Tehillim* (Midrash to Psalms), https://www.sefaria
.org/Midrash_Tehillim.18.29?lang=bi&with=all&lang2=en.

2. As mentioned in previous chapters, some Messianic prophecies
also speak of Messiah bringing justice and ruling all the
nations. I believe that will happen in what some people refer
to as "the end times." If you are interested in digging into
the hope that we can have in Yeshua during those days, you
might want to read my book *Future Hope: A Jewish Christian
Look at the End of the World*, which is available at https://store.
jewsforjesus.org/.

Appendix 1: More Life Stories of Minds Being Opened

1. *El gibor* appears in the Bible in only two places: Isaiah 9:6 (9:5
in the Hebrew) and Isaiah 10:21. It appears in a close form
(*Ha-el ha-gadol ha-gibor*) in three places: Deuteronomy 10:17,
Jeremiah 32:18, and Nehemiah 9:32. Every place clearly refers
to God.

Appendix 2: Theophanies: When God Makes Appearances

1. Arthur G. Patzia and Anthony J. Petrotta, *Pocket Dictionary of
Biblical Studies: Over 300 Terms Clearly and Concisely Defined*
(Downers Grove, IL: IVP Academic, 2002), 116.

2. The Hebrew vowels were written down centuries later, so the
Hebrew text could be read as either *Adoni* or *Adonay*.

3. I am indebted to Gordon J. Wenham, *Genesis 16–50,* Word
Biblical Commentary (Grand Rapids: Zondervan, 2000), for
many of the above insights.

4. Benjamin D. Sommer, *The Bodies of God and the World of Ancient
Israel* (Cambridge: Cambridge University Press, 2009), 40–41.
Hebrew font altered to transliteration.

5. Wenham, *Genesis 16–50*, p. 51.
6. "Angel of the Lord," in *New Bible Dictionary*, 3rd ed. (Downers Grove, IL: InterVarsity Press, 1996), Accordance electronic edition, v. 2.4.
7. *New Bible Dictionary*, "Angel of the Lord."
8. D. N. Freeman et al., *"malāk," Theological Dictionary of the Old Testament*, vol. 8, 321, cited in G. H. Twelftree, "Spiritual Powers," in *New Dictionary of Biblical Theology* (Downers Grove, IL: InterVarsity Press, 2000), Accordance electronic edition, v. 2.2.
9. Whenever I say that God appeared "as" something, we could equally well say that he appeared "in" it. There is a distinction, but either way it is a manifestation of God's person and presence.

Appendix 3: Types: Pictures of Messiah in Scripture
1. Christopher J. H. Wright, *Knowing Jesus through the Old Testament*, 2nd ed. (Downers Grove, IL: InterVarsity Press, 2014), Kindle edition pp. 118–19.
2. For example, in rabbinic tradition Passover imagery is prefigured in the life of Abraham—Abraham's life becomes a *type* of the later Passover—as well in the life of others. And within the Old Testament itself, Passover is used as an image for the return from captivity in Babylon.
3. Based on verses such as John 19:14. Commentator Craig Keener says, "Later rabbis estimated that offerings began earlier on Passover eve, but the slaughter of Passover lambs probably had to continue all day and was finally completed about the time the evening offering was slaughtered, roughly when Jesus died (about 3 p.m.)." In Craig Keener, *The IVP Bible Background Commentary: New Testament* (Downers Grove, IL: InterVarsity Press, 1993), under John 19:6.

4. See Evan Moffic, *What Every Christian Needs to Know about Passover: What It Means and Why It Matters* (Nashville: Abingdon Press, 2014), Kindle edition location 902. For the record, Rabbi Moffic is not a believer in Jesus; he serves as rabbi at Congregation Solel in Highland Park, IL.

5. See for example https://www.chabad.org/holidays/passover/pesach_cdo/aid/5483872/jewish/Why-Red-Wine-at-the-Seder.htm, which also offers additional symbolism for the red wine.

6. Mishnah *Rosh Hashanah* 3:8; italics added.

7. NKJV has "Christ."

8. Sometimes translated as "Sea of Reeds."

9. NKJV has "Christ."

10. Parts of this section were adapted from "The Messiah Would Be a Willing Sacrifice," Jews for Jesus, January 1, 2018, https://jewsforjesus.org/messianic-prophecies/the-messiah-would-be-a-willing-sacrifice.

11. W. Gunther Plaut, *The Torah: A Modern Commentary* (UAHC, 1981), p. 151, n.5. For other sources of this idea, see *Encyclopedia Judaica*, under "Akedah," 2:482; *Canticles [Song of Songs] Rabbah*, I, § 14, I, on 1, 14; f. 12*b* (as cited in C. G. Montefiore and H. M. J. Loewe, *A Rabbinic Anthology* (Cambridge University Press, 2012, orig. 1938), p. 220; *Leviticus Rabbah*, Emor, 29:9, as cited in Montefiore and Loewe, p. 228; *Pirkei deRabbi Eliezer* 31, Sefaria, https://www.sefaria.org/Pirkei_DeRabbi_Eliezer.31.10?lang=bi&with=all&lang2=en; *Shibbolei ha-Leket*, as cited in, e.g., Laura Lieber, *A Vocabulary of Desire: The Song of Songs in the Early Synagogue* (Leiden: Brill, 2014), p. 313 n. 5.

GOD WASN'T FINISHED WORKING IN THE LIVES OF HIS PEOPLE AFTER THE WATERS OF THE RED SEA PARTED.

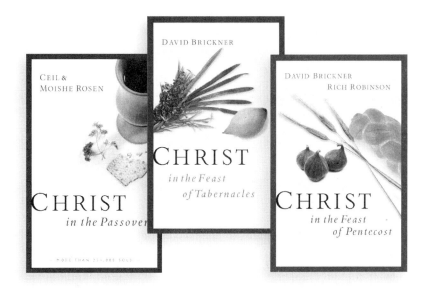

Through *Christ in the Passover*, Ceil and Moishe Rosen trace God's involvement through the history of this holy day—from the first Passover, all the way to the modern Seder. And in the revised editions of this inviting book, the authors show you how the death and resurrection of Jesus the Messiah are forever interwoven with the Passover and its symbolism.

In *Christ in the Feast of Pentecost*, David Brickner and Rich Robinson treat us to the sense of anticipation that "cannot be overstated" as their insightful account of traditions leading up to this holiday unfolds . . . a boy's first haircut, bonfires, sweet treats, artful paper cutting, firstfruits.

In *Christ in the Feast of Tabernacles*, David Brickner will captivate you with the rich imagery of this great festival. From the feast's origins of being celebrated with temporary shelters to modern-day observances—and even its meaning for heaven—you'll be enriched by this fascinating account.

Also available as eBooks

MOODY
Publishers®

From the Word to Life®